The Dichotomy Between Samuel & Saul

An Introspective View of Their Roles
in the Life of King David

Bishop Freddie B. Marshall, Ph.D.

MEMPHIS

The Dichotomy Between Samuel & Saul

KingMaker Publishing, LLC
241 Mill
Suite 102
Memphis, TN 38105

Copyright © 2017 by Bishop Freddie B. Marshall, Ph.D.

All rights reserved. No part of this book may be reproduced, stored in a retrieval system or transmitted in any form or by any means without written permission of the Publisher, excepting brief quotes used in reviews.

All **KingMaker, LLC** Titles, Imprints and Distributed Lines are available at special quantity discounts for bulk purchases for sales promotions, premiums, fund-raising and educational or institutional use.

First KingMaker, LLC Trade Paperback Printing 03-30-2017

ISBN: **978-0-9988108-1-2**

*T*o Jesus Christ through whom I am empowered to share the unsearchable richness of his truth and wonders of his grace, I am because He is.

*T*o my Wife, my Best friend, my heart, and my Life, Azaviea Brown Marshall. There are not enough words in my limited vocabulary to express my love for you. You are the one who completes me, your love for me has healed me. You are to me, the visible manifestation of God's promise to me that He was giving me another chance. You are my theophany. Thank you for your support.

*T*o my children who all represent the drive and need to excel, that has been present in my life because of them. To my sons, I love you, and I believe in all of you, and the greatness of your destinies. To my daughters whose presence competes our family and the lives of my sons, I love you all.

*T*o my parents who have been my strength and support, whose unwavering love has never caused me to feel unloved, but protected. To my brothers and my sister, thank you for being my first best friends.

*T*o the Christ Cathedral Church of Deliverance and Greater Church of Deliverance Incorporated, serving you has not only been my life's mission, it has also been my life's joy. Thank you for allowing me to pour in to your lives, and to watch you grow by grace daily

…..and to the memory of and presence of my spiritual fathers, and mentors, your impression in my life have blessed me, my family, and my ministry.

Table of Contents

Introduction 1

Chapter 1 11

The Mourning Prophet and a Disappointed God............ 11

Chapter 2 31

I May Not Be First, But I'm Next.. 31

Chapter 3 51

God Said You Can Do Better Than This.............................. 51

Chapter 4 67

You're about to be Promoted by Jealousy 67

Chapter 5 81

The Difference is in His Anointing............................ 81

Introduction

For years the Spirit of the Lord has dealt with me about the personage of King David. I have become a student of the process by which the Lord guides David, becoming personally acquainted with his flaws and successes. It has become apparent to me that God chooses not only the vessel for His divine will to be done on the earth, but He also chooses those who serve in pivotal roles of support. I often teach those around me to be comfortable in the starring role of the saga called life; it is the only real opportunity each individual has to be in the leading role. Yet the more I give myself to study and preparation for my next-life performance, the more I am drawn to the need for a supporting cast. The Author and Finisher of our faith vehemently declares He knows the thoughts He has about us, and those thoughts will bring us to His closing act, our final episode.

I have observed a contrast and yet continuity of such roles in the lives of the prophet Samuel and Saul, Israel's first king. Though each is, in his own life, the main character, they are both intricately and intimately woven in the development of David, God's chosen vessel. The cooperation of Samuel in the introduction of David to his destiny is in stark contrast to the duplicity of Saul in his futile attempts to destroy David. David needs and God periodically uses both supporting characters to secure His plan of success for this founder of the bloodline of the Messiah, this shadow of the Christ who is to come some twenty-eight generations later.

Samuel is the prophet who speaks in the life of David from his initial public introduction in 1 Samuel 10:11–12, through the many challenges of his maturation, until he is prepared to ascend to the throne of Israel. Saul, on the other hand, is the king (spiritual father) who directly benefits the most from the hand of David. Yet Saul's immaturity and lack of identity causes him to become the nemesis to his own support. Instead of fathering David and loving him as a father should, Saul allows his own intimidation by David's presence, potential, and praise to become the justification for incendiary remarks that wound the reputation of David but build his character. It is through Saul's attempts to destroy David before the king's court that love and reverence for David are accelerated and turned to deference in all who observe his love toward his thorn.

The ability to serve while under attack became a defining quality in the life of David. Saul was at times out of control. He knew how to scheme against the young servant-leader because David was vulnerable in his heart—his desire to serve Saul was beyond words. So the two dominant characteristics of David, the worshipper and the warrior, are revealed in his service to Saul. Saul benefits from both aspects of the king in waiting, yet it is through David's willingness to serve that Saul attempts time and time again to destroy David.

Samuel's role in these times of conflict becomes extremely valuable to David. The consistency of Samuel's voice, the integrity of his heart toward God, and his diligence in his assignment on earth are pivotal not only in the development, but in the deployment of David's reign.

We all must learn to deal with both the Samuels and the Sauls in our lives. When I think of Samuel, I think of the helper who builds David, speaks into and over the life of David, and causes David to walk into himself. Everyone has to find a Samuel who is so connected to God that as he speaks, he speaks words of life into your existence. What he speaks awakens your being. Everything about you becomes alive, vibrant, well, and even potent.

We must also reckon with Saul. Saul represents what should have been a blessing to you, what sometimes you've given yourself over to by way of service and by way of honor. Instead of celebrating you and releasing the potency of his words over your life, Saul speaks words to destroy or discredit you. Every ministry gift, no matter what you are assigned to do, will have to reckon with both Samuel and Saul. Every ministry gift will need both Samuel and Saul.

I want to deal with the dichotomy between the two supporting characters in order to build you up. Saul and Samuel are each necessary. God has given me five specific themes around the relationship of Samuel and Saul.

1) A Mourning Prophet and a Disappointed God (1 Samuel 15:35)

As God began to speak to me about this particular theme, my heart was pulled. There are tearstains on my pages because I really heard the heart of God and pulled myself into some sense of check. Has God ever spoken to you and made you look at yourself—not at anyone else, but yourself? I began to say, "God, whatever I do, I do not want to disappoint you."

I will disappoint people; I have. As long as I'm living and in this body of clay, there will be some things I say, some actions, and some demeanors that will bring about a sense of disappointment in people. Leadership teaches you that pleasing everyone is impossible. Compromise, from my perspective, means that someone lost or gave up something in order for a common ground to be reached. A recent situation with the government is a clear example of compromise. Something was given up for the debt ceiling to be raised and for the bill that was signed by the president to go into effect.

God began to deal with me, and we are going to get into this particular subject in depth, because we waste a lot of time mourning what God has rejected, as did Samuel.

2) I May Not Be First, But I'm Next (1 Samuel 16:11–12)

This chapter deals with the relationship that David has with his father, Jesse. Jesse is very much responsible for many of the imbalances that exist within David as a man. Jesse was not a spiritual father to David, but he was David's biological father. It was his responsibility to cover his son, to cover his child, and there were times when David was left uncovered. A majority of David's dysfunction is a result of his father's inadequacy.

Jesse had no regard for David, as can be seen clearly in 1 Samuel 16:11–12. When Samuel goes down to Jesse's house to anoint the next king, Jesse parades all but one of his sons before Samuel. When Samuel asks Jesse if Samuel has seen all of his sons,

Jesse replies, in effect, "Well, there is one more. He is not what you really want, but he's out tending sheep."

Sometimes the rejection you live through and the spirit of rejection that constantly visits you is a result of rejection you felt in the house in which you were raised. Your own blood can give you so much rejection that you would rather be accepted by what is wrong than wait on what is right. Many of us are stuck in that dilemma.

This book is really written from my own pain, discomfort, and dysfunction, because sometimes your personal struggles make you a mouthpiece. This is why we must not live our lives trying to hide all of our dysfunctions. The power of who you are and what God wants to use comes out of what you failed to do right. Do not allow others to judge and tell you that you are eligible only if you crossed every "t" and dotted every "i." No, you are eligible because you are God's choice. Good, bad, or indifferent; right or wrong; doing it or not doing it; when you know who you are, then you recognize that God uses it all to make you.

We are dealing with a generation that is trying its best to reach God, but the spirit of pseudo-apostolic fathers, who want to play perfect with unresolved issues, are not being a strength to this generation. I was speaking with Bishop Hearns of Littlerock, California, and he asked, "What are we going to do?"

"Bishop, we've got to find fathers," I replied.

Bishop Hearns is seventy-eight years old and is just now coming into himself. He said to me, "Bishop, the prophetic words you spoke four or five years ago, I'm just now walking into." He is seventy-eight years old and just realizing how to be a father, seventy-eight years old and just walking into an apostolic anointing, trying to find his way.

This bishop is an intelligent man working as an engineer for the government, a man who became the mayor of the city he lives in, yet God had me speaking into his life. He said, "Man of God, where are the voices that will bridge the gap between the generations? Because if we do not bridge the gap, the church herself will lose her potency to really make a difference in the world."

The world is quaking and literally crumbling at the core because the church is not together. We would rather play politics with each other than go before God prostrate and say to Him, "God, help me."

3) God Said You Can Do Better Than This

When the Lord spoke this to me, I began to tremble. It put me in a place where I recognized that settling and not waiting is a challenge in this generation. I began to recollect all of the things I've settled for in my life. All of the not-good-enough situations that I submitted myself to because I couldn't wait for what God had for me. All of the not-good-enough relationships that I embraced, all of the not-good-enough decisions that I made because if God was saying, "I'm not giving it to you yet," I just settled for what was available.

In 1 Samuel 15:28, God says that He is taking the kingdom from Saul. God says something through the prophet that I've never seen before. He says that He's giving the kingdom to somebody better than Saul. I don't want to be to in the place where God looks to me and says, "There is somebody better than you."

This is what we have to understand: God never finds somebody better because of what we may have done wrong or the mistakes we've made. He does it when we no longer hear Him. He does it when we no longer submit to His voice. It's when you no longer are saying, "Lord, You be my guide," that God will reject you. God rejects Saul. God says to him, "I took you from nothing and gave you My chosen people, and all you could bring yourself to do was let your ego trip you up."

We must be careful that as God elevates, blesses, uses, and calls us into places that we've never heretofore been, we don't get so wonderful that God looks at us and says, "I've found somebody better than you." Lord, whatever You do in my life, keep me humble at Your feet. I believe that the trouble I must go through, the things I must endure, are all God's way of saying, "I'm using you, but don't ever get so cocky as to think that it's all about you." Your gift isn't about you. The anointing upon your life is His anointing. None of us have an anointing. What we do, we do through His anointing. Christ is the Anointed One, and it is His anointing. We must protect His anointing upon our lives.

4) You're About to be Promoted by Jealousy

I'm tired of a generation that talks about haters but puts them in the wrong perspective. You need every hater you've got. Comedian Katt Williams has sense enough to know this. Katt Williams said that if you have ten haters, you should work on having a hundred haters by the end of the month. When you get to a hundred, you need to see what you can do to get to five hundred by the next month.

Now if Katt Williams has sense enough to know that haters only push you, then why is the church sitting around acting like a hater is someone sent to shut you down? When you have haters in your life, that's an indication that somebody wants to be what you already are. And the beauty of what you already are is that you know that's not all you're going to be.

5) The Difference is in His Anointing

Stop trying to flow in something you're not anointed for. When God puts His hand on us, we are empowered. When He takes His hand off of us, we are no longer empowered. That is the tragedy of

The Dichotomy Between Samuel & Saul

people not knowing when to move, not knowing when to change, not knowing when to sit down. The Scripture says the Spirit of the Lord is upon me because He hath anointed me. When the anointing lifts, I need to sit down.

If I can train this generation in anything, please allow me to help you be a little wiser than the folk who are before us and don't have sense enough to know when it's time to move out of the way. Maybe that's why the pressure is on us so. Maybe that's why we're under such a heavy load now. God really doesn't want us to become so comfortable that we are locked into something and can't move to the next place. In pastoring over these last five years and seeing the number of people who have come into this ministry, one of the things that has been really challenging to me is I have a hard time getting people to their next assignment. The challenge is not that I don't see it. The challenge is they don't know how to move. Let me help you.

You came from XYZ church in QRS city in ABC state. In that church, you were chief broom carrier. You did it so well, they gave you a broom carrier appreciation service. You were excellent at carrying that broom. But God then called you here. When you got here, we already had a chief broom carrier. Our chief broom carrier is still assigned to carry the broom. When we look at her, we see the broom-carrying anointing on her.

As the pastor who is the chief seer in this house, I say to you, "I need for you to look toward the mop ministry."

You say to me, "I've been doing broom ministry for twenty years, and I just feel like I'm called to the broom."

But here broom ministry is well covered, and we have a mop ministry deficiency. We ask you to look toward the mop ministry, and you say no. So every time we look for you, you are over near the broom ministry, trying to give instruction to an already functioning part of the body. Nothing more challenging than trying ...

I would much rather grow a church with new converts than you seasoned people. Because new converts at least come in saying, "Whatever it is the Lord wants me to do, I'm ready to do it." Those of you who have been somewhere else, and somebody told you how wonderful you are, it's hard to get you to see your next assignment.

That is where the Body of Christ is stuck today. We are stuck in our last assignment. Why are we stuck there? It's comfortable, it's what we know, and we're familiar with it. But what we really ought to be doing is saying to God, "Don't let me get so comfortable in broom ministry that I miss my mop-carrying potential." That's a challenge.

Chapter 1

The Mourning Prophet and a Disappointed God

"And Samuel came no more to see Saul until the day of his death. Nevertheless Samuel mourned for Saul and the Lord repented that He had made Saul King over Israel" (1 Samuel 15:35).

Grief and disappointment are both very strong emotions. They are, as a matter of fact, two emotions that can become very easy gateways to other dominant spirits operating within one's life. The text before us reveals the power of these two emotions as exhibited through the prophet Samuel and the Creator, God our Father.

To view God as disappointed may be an uncomfortable perception to many, because we are most comfortable seeing God as the Sovereign Deity who is clear on the predestined places He has for His children. However, in this text, we are introduced to the disappointment of God. I don't ever want to be the cause of God's disappointment. Yet we are always complicit in this, because our sinful exploits—not our sinful nature—disappoint God.

God was disappointed in Saul. God had given Saul the opportunity to become what no man before him had achieved—to be king over God's chosen people. Historically, we understand that the need for a king was more a cry from the people than a need from God. Yet this loving and caring God always desired to provide the very best for His children. Saul rose from total obscurity to prominence, and like many others before him, he couldn't balance his calling and assignment with the egotistical overstatement of his own importance.

Scripture states that God repented for making Saul king over Israel. To repent is greater than just to quit, stop, or change. That's the watered-down version of the etymology of the word. God didn't just quit, stop, or change his mind about Saul; God turned away from Saul. *God, don't ever turn away from me!*

Why did God repent (turn away from) Saul?
        1)   Saul felt God first.
        2)   Saul failed to recognize the will of God.
        3)   Saul rejected God's instructions.
        4)   Saul feared the people.
        5)   Saul ignored the warnings of the prophet.

God does not change His mind—what He says, He means; what He intends, He carries out. As much as God does not change His own mind, we do change His mind! Hezekiah changed God's mind when he turned his face to the wall, causing God to send back the prophet Isaiah and adding fifteen more years to his life.

Many great leaders have missed the mark because they choose not to hear the voice of God above their own egocentric ways and feelings. It is dangerous when a leader leads from autopilot rather than from prayer life—not prayer just for the things needed in ministry or for those who ask for prayer, but a prayer life that calls for consecration and dedication. A prayer life speaks to the need for God's divine providence to direct our lives, not our own wills, no matter how admirable they may be.

Every time I think of this and look at this theme, I start to shake within myself. What's really taking place in this text is that God is telling you if you don't move on, you will be stuck trying to minister to what He has rejected. How much time, energy …

My spiritual brother posed a question to me that really put me in a mode of thinking. He said to me, "Bishop Marshall, how much more of yourself are you willing to lose trying to help something that can't be helped?" You've got to come to the place in your life where you go into a mode of obedient preservation. That means when you sense that God has removed His hand from something, you don't take His anointing into that thing and try to make work what God is no longer working with. We do it not just with churches or ministries, but also with interpersonal relationships.

God has said to us time and time again to move on, get up out of that, go on about your business, or go to the next assignment, but because we are trying to be loyal—to our own detriment—we stay stuck in something that God has put His hand on no more. The glory has been lifted off that thing. When the glory lifts, you are in jeopardy of being in the posture of God looking at you and saying, "I told you to move, and if you don't move, I'm not going to use you."

Loyalty is beautiful—but not to the extent that I lose out with God. The spirit of Ichabod is on some stuff, and you better know how to discern where the spirit of Ichabod is. When God's glory has lifted, you better know how to get in your car and go in the opposite direction. I'm trying to get the saints to see this. Really, what has to happen is that you have to stay in tune with the voice of God to know.

I've said for years that I want to be where God is, not where God was. A lot of times, we can't even move from where God was to where God is, because we're trying to be loyal for the wrong reason. If the day comes when you don't sense God where you are, your next responsibility is to find out where He is. If you don't know where God is, you don't know what God is saying.

God spoke to Samuel and said, "I've rejected Saul." The dichotomy that existed between Samuel and Saul was that Samuel stayed with God after Saul walked away from God. The danger in trying to maintain closeness with somebody who's no longer in communion with God is that when God comes for that person, you don't want to be in the room. I love you, but if the glory has lifted, I don't want you preaching to me. I don't want you laying hands on me. I don't want you speaking into my life. If the glory has lifted, you're not going to transfer your spirit of Ichabod to me.

I've come to the conclusion that as a priest, I have that responsibility first to myself, second to my family, and third to my church. I cannot drag you where God is not. I cannot drag you where God refuses to go. This thing that we have is because we think we are really anointed—we think God is really with us.

You are not so anointed that you can change an atmosphere that God has rejected. You can't carry His anointing into an atmosphere. I don't care how anointed with the spirit of David y'all are. You can get on the keyboard, organ, drums, or bongos, or grab a tambourine, but if God has rejected the atmosphere, you won't get anything going there. Nobody will be delivered; nobody will be saved. Folks will jump, shout, and move to the beat of the music, but nobody will change.

It's a dangerous thing to carry God's anointing into an atmosphere that He has rejected. According to Scripture, Samuel did not go to visit Saul anymore until the day of his death. Beware when God moves the prophetic out of your midst, because where there is no prophecy, there is no future.

Where I live, I've found a restaurant that I really like—a little Chinese restaurant with really good food. I went one Saturday. They give you fortune cookies at the end of your meal. Everybody got their fortune cookies, so at the table, everyone was engulfed in the activity of reading their fortunes. When they got around to me, I cracked mine open, but there was no fortune in it. I ate the cookie and went about my business. I went back the next Saturday, and there was again no fortune in my cookie.

The enemy started trying to speak to me. "See, nothing is going to happen for you." Everybody else read, "Next week's going to be great," or "Good things are coming your way"—all that good stuff—and there was nothing in my fortune. The enemy told me, "Everybody's got good fortune coming but you." I went to my car, and I felt something go up my leg. My mind went back to this book.

Part of Saul's problem was that he started consorting with witches. God said to Saul, "I speak to you through my prophets; my prophets have told you what to do." When Saul no longer wanted to hear the true prophets of God, he consorted with witches. Saul conjured up the witches of Endor, and they started speaking what Saul wanted to hear.

God spoke to me on my way to the car and said, "The reason there was nothing in your cookie is because I talk to you." I want God to speak to me, not witches. Some of you better watch who's speaking to you and speaking over your life. God sent me to tell you you've got some witches in your ear. It's a dangerous thing when you allow witches.

A witch is a spirit of manipulation. A witch is a spirit of control—a spirit that wants to control you. Watch people who don't teach you how to think freely. You don't want to be under a leader who has to tell you every move to make, when to make it, and what you can't do. The Devil is a lie. I want to learn how to hear from God. My responsibility is not to teach you to hear me, but to teach you to hear God through me.

You better learn, if you don't learn nothing else, how to hear God. The day is going to come when God is going to still my voice. You ain't God. Ain't nobody God but God. You better learn how to hear His voice. Once you hear His voice, you will not follow another.

Samuel is a powerful man of God because Samuel sees himself as important enough in the plan of God not to get caught up. You have to understand the scenario. Saul is king. Most people today want to get close to power, but I'm here to tell you that instead of trying to get close to position, you better try to get close to glory. Saul had the power as king, but the glory rested on Samuel. You have to bring yourself to a place where you say, "I ain't trying to get close to no certain person. I'm trying to get where the glory is. I just want to be where the glory is."

Samuel doesn't visit Saul anymore until the day of his death. The Bible declares to us that Samuel then goes into a season of mourning. If God's going to be able to trust you in this next season, you have to detach yourself from being so close to personalities that you miss your assignment.

I watched it here in February when we started going through transitions from music ministry through other facets of the ministry. Since February, we have been in major transition, and some folk got messed up because they were more connected to personality than to their assignments. Let me help you with this. Don't ever get so caught up in personality that you don't any longer value your assignment. I can be close to you. So close that we are thick as thieves. So close that we become almost Siamese in our connection. But I've got to put in perspective the closeness. Sometimes we're this close because our assignments intertwine. But if God ever changes the assignment, calling you that way and calling me this way, we can't go connected. We can't go trying to hold on to each another.

Don't get so caught up in the personality that you let the personality keep you from the assignment. I love you, but I have to let you go. I love you, we had some good times, but if God is calling you west and He's calling me east, then I have to take on the attitude of Abraham. Abraham said to Lot, "You choose where you're going. Whatever you choose, I'll go the other direction, because what God's gon' do in both of us is greater than us trying to be in each other's face all the time."

I love you, but I got to move on. I love you, but I got to go on about my assignment. I love you, but I got to let you go.

A lot of folk are in love and let love keep them from education. "I'm so in love, I don't want to go to college." You better go. If it's real love, it'll be there after you get that degree, after they put that hood around your neck, after put that tassel on your hat and you walk.

Stop letting your future be held up because you don't know how to let go of personalities. If you are really the kind of person who can make friends, then you can make friends anywhere. You will have folk you didn't think liked you doing stuff for you, because when you have a friendly persona, when you have a friendly demeanor, people will just come to you.

You can put me anywhere. Put me anywhere, Lord, anywhere but jail in Jesus's name. That's one place I do not want to be used. And prison. I don't want to be used there either. I can make friends, but I would not make any there because I wouldn't be there long. But the point is this. If you are friendly, you can find you some friends. As a matter of fact, you'll find some friends who can provoke you to become a better you.

A person might say, "We've been friends since we were in preschool." That's really admirable, but you ain't made no friends since then? What that means is you only got speaking to you that one voice. It's the folk I met in college who really helped to shape me. It's amazing—I went to college with people from my high school, and we didn't all remain close. You want to know why? We were in an environment that engendered some evolution.

I feel sorry for you if you just hang around church people all the time. "I just want to be around the saints." You have nobody in your life but the saints? I envy those of you who work secular jobs. I really envy you to an extent because you have opportunity to interact.

One of the things that I regret was never pledging to a fraternity in college. Our discipline manual said that we couldn't belong to any outside secret societies, but I sure wish I hadn't paid that any attention. You want to know why? Because I want to be able to go somewhere and interact with somebody who ain't got nothing to do with church.

There is more to me than what I know about the Scripture. I'm intelligent. I know how to carry on a conversation. When you are with the saints, you don't get that, because if they are not talking Jesus, they are talking drama. I don't want to talk either of those things all day, not even

Jesus, because there is more to me than that. I have a political side. I'm very political. I'm very opinionated. I love to debate. I think I can answer all of the questions on *Jeopardy!*

So there is more to me. If I am only talking to saints, I get tired of hearing, "I'm just waiting on the Lord." I want to talk to some people who ain't waiting on Him; they already got Him. I'm being real. I really want to go play golf, I want to bowl, I want to go to the beach, I want to ride a roller coaster.

Bishop Gardner and I were down in Atlanta at Six Flags, and we were not on the roller coaster hollering "Jesus!" We were just hollering. Six Flags has a roller coaster that takes your picture. We looked like night and day coming down the roller coaster. We walked in Six Flags, laughing and talking, and we were not quoting Scripture.

Please don't be so one-sided that all you are is somebody who can exist in the church world. If you are Kingdom, there is more to you than the church. You ought to be able to sit with kings and presidents and be recognized as a voice to be reckoned with. Stop looking for people who are only somebody Jesus.

When I started back up TBS a couple of years ago, our lesson was on diversity—teaching our young people to be diverse. You know what their assignment was the first night? Go home and make friends with somebody on Facebook from another country. And they were floored. I said to them the next week, "Go to school and make friends with somebody from another culture." And they were floored. What they discovered was there was somebody looking at them, wanting to know about them just as much as they wanted to learn about others.

You have to be able to take advantage of certain opportunities. Stop being one-sided. Black Theater Festival is in town? Go see something. Have a moment someplace. Seeing gospel plays is all cute because you know eventually they gon' start singing a song, crowd gon' start moving, hands gon' go up. Expose yourself to something different. Find an opera, go to it. Go to a jazz concert.

We were having dinner the other night, and Carlton started singing a Prince song, but he was singing it in Beyoncé's style. Beyoncé had performed a cover of a Prince song.

I said, "That's Prince."

And Carlton said, "Oh yeah, he was on stage with her."

"On stage with her? No, she was on stage with *him*. It's his song."

You don't know nothing but one music. I need for you to be well-rounded. Ain't nothing like when I go on YouTube and watch Roberta Flack sit at the piano and sing "Killing Me Softly." Lauryn Hill ain't got nothing on Roberta. Like when I watch Aretha Franklin sit at the piano. I ain't talking Aretha singing "Amazing Grace." I'm talking about Aretha singing "Bridge Over Troubled Water," which you'd think she owns until you hear Simon and Garfunkel sing it because they're the ones who wrote it. I thought Chris Brown was doing something in that movie *This Christmas* when he was singing "Try a Little Tenderness"—until I found Otis Redding. Otis was wearing it out. I said, "Chris Brown better go somewhere and sit down, because Otis owns that."

You have to have some diversity. I ain't talking about hard rap where they're belittling anybody or demeaning anybody. I'm talking about you having a sense of diversity. Don't get stuck with just one side of you being developed.

Go to lunch with your coworkers. You don't have to say what they are saying or do what they are doing. If you are strong enough, you'll become the center of the conversation. It may be a witnessing moment. It may be a moment for them to realize, as much as you don't club with them and party with them, you do have a sense of humor.

Samuel mourns for Saul. Samuel mourns for him because there is nothing worse than a missed opportunity that you'll never get again. Sometimes I'm crying because I realize I just missed an opportunity that'll never come back. Opportunities don't always come around. Stop missing moments. The Kingdom is about moments. You cannot live your life missing moments that may not ever come around again.

Satan's goal is to keep you so stressed that you miss Kingdom moments. We are so stressed that we can't get nothing done. You're so stressed you can't even get a clear thought. So you have to divest yourself. I'm learning that we have to stop living our lives with so much distress. We have to learn how to de-stress.

Let me tell you what I'm learning how to do: divest myself of myself. Divorce myself from my emotions. I get to writing and things start flowing when I divorce myself from my emotions. My emotions are out of whack because they're Satan's way of keeping me really bound and in poverty. When I'm free, I can make some money come my way. Money be looking for me when I'm free. But when I'm stressed, I can't find no money.

You have to divorce yourself of your emotions. Move yourself away from your emotions. Say to your emotions, "Okay, ain't nothing gon' change. Let's do this. Let's just start it. Let's try it. Y'all ready?" By the time work closes at five o'clock, divorce yourself from worrying about stuff that can't be resolved 'til nine o'clock the next morning. Which means from five to nine, that stuff ain't got no time, it ain't in my thought pattern, I ain't thinking about it, I ain't worried about it. Want to know why? Because there is nothing I can do about it right now.

So let me give myself to something creative. Let me give myself to something fruitful and productive. Let me think about what I want to do. I want to go see *The Smurfs*. Just want to go see them. They're at the movies right now, and before they leave, I'm going. I'm gon' take the kids as my excuse, but I want to see *The Smurfs*. That's my generation. I grew up on the Smurfs.

The Bible says that Saul missed God and Samuel mourned for Saul. I'm not gon' spend the next season of my life crying over what somebody else doesn't care about. You are crying over something that somebody else doesn't care about. He done dogged you out and you still crying. Take on his spirit. He don't care, you don't either.

People say, "He hurt me." I'm not just talking in no relationship either. We say that in church: "They hurt me." But yet they go on about their business, sitting up in O'Charley's, Golden Corral, or Friday's, eating Jack Daniels wings ... that's the saints' way of trying to get a li'l something. They order Jack Daniels wings, Jack Daniels shrimp, and a Jack Daniels pork chop, but they don't have sense enough to know that when the kitchen put the heat on it, that burned all the alcohol out of it. Then they start sitting up, rocking like they really got something in their system.

Stop worrying about what somebody else didn't care about. I'm not worrying about folk who don't want to come to church. If you don't come to church, you don't care, why am I crying over it? I'm in church. I'm hearing the Word. I'm under the anointing.

If they fire you, then your focus needs to be, "Where do I go from here?" First place you need to go is the unemployment office and apply for unemployment, because them bills coming around next month and the creditors don't want to hear they fired you. What creditors want to hear is when you're going to pay.

We spend too much of our time mourning over what somebody else doesn't care about. Why is Samuel mourning over Saul's recklessness? Here's the answer: the Kingdom is at stake. When the Kingdom is at stake, it requires some attention. I'm only going to mourn long enough to pull God to move. After God moves, I'm not gon' be stuck in somebody else's mistake.

Stop letting people drag you into their stuff. They get out of it, and you're stuck in it. If your spouse don't want you talking to nobody, don't get stuck in that. That's jealousy. That's the kind of jealousy that no matter what's going on, they gon' always have a problem with it. You can be talking to your own momma, they gon' be mad. You must pull yourself into a place of truly understanding this.

The Bible says that Samuel did not visit Saul anymore until the day of Saul's death. Samuel mourned, and God repented that He had ever made Saul king. Ain't nothing worse than when your drama pushes God to resent what He's done for you.

Say that somebody is able to sing, and the MC (we call them presiders today) says, "Oh, so-and-so is here and he can sing, let's have him to come up and bless us."

The person gets up slowly, and he walks over to the musician and says, "I don't know what I'm going to do, so just follow me. Put me in A-flat. I'm gon' try to do a little bit of this song ... y'all pray with me." Then he sings after he does all of that, and he's turned you off. Then he gets mad at you. "Y'all ain't getting with me." Why? He didn't want to minister. So we don't want him ministering to us.

Don't ever get to the point where you are so about yourself that God looks at you and repents giving you the gift. If I could sing like some of you …

This is what Shirley Caesar said once; I heard her say it out of her own mouth. The Caravans came to Durham. She was sitting in the back. She wrote a note that said, "Let little Shirley Caesar sing." She gave it to the usher. The usher took it to Albertina Walker. Albertina read it. They didn't know at the time that Shirley sent her own note.

If you can do it, nobody should have to beg you to do it. If I could sing like some of you, I would be setting up concerts. I've got my own platform, got my own mic, got Mike, KJ, and Third. Tonight at seven o'clock, I'm gon' be having a concert. Y'all got some new material for me? I wouldn't be redoing other people's stuff. I'd be doing some fresh stuff.

The Bible says God repented that He ever made Saul king. Some people can't handle promotion, so they can't stand to be blessed. Watch it when you become so cocky. The things that I can do, nobody has ever had to ask me to do twice. Never. I'm preaching. I'm a preacher. I'm mature enough now to recognize that every call is not for me to answer, because they're not all my assignments, but I ain't struggling with preaching.

I was going to New York, and I assigned Lady Marshall to preach Sunday morning and Sunday evening. She asked, "Why I got to do both? Let Bishop Gardner do one."

I said, "You're a preacher, aren't you? You preach."

"But I don't how to preach no two times in one day."

"I didn't either until I did it."

Then you say, Lord, okay, try me three times in one day. Then you say, Lord, see how many times a week I can preach. A man's gift makes room for him.

As a preacher, I ain't worried when people are calling me. I am worried when ain't nobody calling me. It's a thing I'm sent to the Kingdom to do. If there ain't nobody looking for me to do it, nobody calling me, nobody searching for me, nobody wanting me? Something is wrong.

That's why I don't understand how you can't find Sunday school teachers. I taught Sunday school before I was a preacher. When I became a preacher, teaching Sunday school was a joy. As a preacher, it was my opportunity to get out of my spirit what was in there.

I've been preaching ever since God called me to preach. You want to know why? Because preaching was slipping out of me even before I became a preacher. People would say stuff like, "You sound like a preacher." "You look like a preacher." "You act like a preacher." Before the title was given to me, I was preaching. This generation makes me real nervous because we got to beg preachers. I ain't never seen nothing like it in my life.

KJ texted me at six o'clock the other morning. I said, "Lord Jesus, something is wrong with him. I know he's new, Lord, and he's excited, but the wrath of God is about to come down on him." Then I read his text.

You know what he texted me? "Could you please make sure that you pick me up because I want to go to ministers' meeting." Ever since KJ's been here, he's been saying, "I know I'm called. I just need somebody to help me get into it."

You think I'm going to beg preachers? I got somebody who's up at six trying to learn to preach. You think I'm gon' beg you, Elder? Think I'm gon' beg you, Pastor? I'll work with somebody who just wants to learn, because I can pour into somebody who wants to learn.

KJ's got a zeal, it just wasn't according to knowledge. Knowledge would have told him to wait 'til about nine thirty. That's when my Jesus anointing kicks in. Six o'clock, I was still dreaming. It was a Monday, too. He was trying to get a ride for Saturday on Monday. Somebody is this excited about what's on the inside, and you think we gon' waste time begging? I'll give a mic to a prostitute and let her sing before I beg you to come from the back row when you should've been on the praise team.

The Bible says that God repented. When I looked at that, I started to say, "God, whatever I have done" —and I have done some stuff. I have done some stuff since God called me. Do you hear me? Some stuff I have been guilty of, but I have prayed the prayer— "God, I don't care what I've done or what I might do, I don't ever want to do nothing that's gon' make You change Your mind about who You called me to be. Uphold me with Thy Spirit, and whatever You do, Lord, don't take Your anointing away from me. I don't want to lose Your anointing."

You all know you've done some things that, if it were left up to man, would disqualify you from the service of the Lord. But if you recognize that, then I can show you what makes David a man after God's own heart. I can prove to you he lied, I can prove to you he was a philanderer. I can prove to you he wasn't a good father. I can show all of this stuff to you in the Scripture. What makes David a man after God's own heart? I believe that no matter what David did, he knew how to get to God and say, "Create within me a clean heart."

You can't pray that prayer too many times without God doing it. You don't pray, "Create within me a clean heart," until you are to the place where you can admit you have a dirty one. There's stuff God used me to do, and I recognize that He used me in spite of my heart. But He used me because I was on the cusp of saying, "Create within me a clean heart."

You can't blackmail me because I done got to God long before you could make it news, long before it could start circulating in your family, long before it could start circulating among your friends.

I put this on Facebook and I didn't get no responses; I thought that was interesting. My title was "An Open Confession and Repentance." So I thought everybody would read it because they'd think I'm gon' confess something. You know the saints love tea. I had to confess.

I got a text from one of my spiritual daughters from Nashville, Tennessee. She testified to me and said, "Bishop, I just left the doctor. I'm completely blind in one eye and I only have 30% vision in the other. I'm living in a home with somebody I don't believe loves me anymore, and I want to quit. I want to die. I want to give up. I thought it only right for me to write you to let you know that at least I appreciate all you taught me."

I sent her back a text message. I wasn't led to call her. I wasn't led to try to find her. I sent her back a text message, and I said, "You can't quit, you can't die, and you probably want to know why, because your situation sounds like it's worthy of that. Out of all the stuff I taught you, I never taught you how to give up."

When I stopped texting and moved on to something else, it hit me. That's what birthed my posting on Facebook. I realized I needed to apologize to all my spiritual and biological children and let them know that out of all the stuff they get from me, the one thing I will not pass on is how to quit. Want to know why? Because I don't know how. I don't know how to quit. I've tried. I've tried to walk away from this city, and God wouldn't let me. I've tried to throw in the towel, and it just kept coming back. I can't teach you something I don't know.

So you can't quit because I don't know how to teach you that. You can't throw in the towel, you can't walk away, you can't give up, because you got my DNA in you. When I passed my DNA to you, I passed along a stubbornness that will make you keep coming when the whole city is laughing at you. Make you keep showing up, make you keep going to K & W when you know that if you walk in, the room will get silent and folk start whispering, "There he is."

So you're kind of stuck. You're stuck with an inability to give up. You might change assignments, you might go and do something different, but you can't quit.

In 1990, on February third, I started the ministry. This is how I remember the date. February 3, 1990, I stopped up at 1600 North Liberty Street at Gilmore's Funeral Home, because they gave me the money for the first altar communion set that I bought. They donated it.

When I went in, Mrs. Gilmore said to me, "Freddie, don't let us down."

Jerry, her son, said to me, "Whatever you do, be consistent. Don't start a church and a few months later stop it."

For twenty-one years without fail, I've stood up every week because I ain't got no quit in me. I ain't got no give-up in me. Scandalized, business put out, but I keep going.

Lost some things and a lot of people along the way, but I don't know how to stop.

> So when I say,
> A charge to keep I have,
> A God to glorify,
> A never-dying soul to save,
> And fit it for the sky.
> To serve the present age,
> My calling to fulfill:
> O may it all my powers engage
> To do my Master's will!
> Arm me with jealous care,
> As in Thy sight to live;
> And O Thy servant, Lord, prepare
> A strict account to give!

When I talk like that, I ain't talking as no little fly-by-night who woke up one morning and decided I wanted to do this. I was fine where I was. When I write and talk out about Samuel and Saul, it ain't something I picked up because I watched TBN late one night. I lived it.

What am I trying to share with you? I shared it with my daughter just the other day. Embrace who God is calling you to be. Forget those things which are behind you and press toward the things which are ahead of you. Will people try to hold your past against you? I'm a witness they will. But I'm also a witness that you can outlive what they want to say. After a while, they will stop defining you by what you did, and they'll start saying when you walk in the room, "Here comes the man God has blessed."

When I walk in the room, I want people to say, "Here comes the man in whom there is no guile." That's my prayer. That's why I'm going to show up some places, I'm going to stop by some places, I'm going to be visible some places, because I may not be first, but I'm next.

Why? God said you can do better than that because His anointing makes a difference. That's how you build legacy. You build a generation of people who don't know how to give up. Who don't make their hurts, their pains, their disappointments, and even their failures an excuse for not doing. Somewhere along the way, they start looking at themselves, saying, "God, if You go with me, I'll go. If You called me, I recognize that he whom You've called, You've justified and qualified."

I pray that you become what God has called you to become. I know it's been rough, and I wish my prognosis was that it's going to be smooth sailing from here. But the truth of the matter is, we both gon' see some more troublesome days. Trouble won't last always. We gon' get enough done that when trouble comes, we'll be able to coast off of what we've done until we can get back on our feet.

Chapter 2
I May Not Be First, But I'm Next

I want to release this word and build encouragement in the hearts of God's people.

A young man that the Lord blessed me to encounter over the last couple of years is a member of a church in another state. We have talked about spiritual things, we have talked about his business pursuits, and we have had these discussions over the last year or so. He sent me a message, as he does almost every day, sending blessings and greetings. He said to me, "Bishop, I've been thinking about something, and I wanted to know if I could run it by you."

I texted back, "Sure."

He said, "I have been praying about asking you to be a mentor to me in my life for what it is God has called me to do."

My response to him was, "I would be honored to be so and to serve in that capacity in your life."

He told me he felt better now that he had gotten that off of his heart. It's something he had been praying about and thinking about and just didn't know how to approach. I assured him that I take it very seriously.

I want to share this story with you because it ties in to where we will go in this lesson. This young man, I believe, is pastored and covered in his home church. Yet there is a connection that he feels to my voice. It doesn't mean that there is not sufficient covering. A lot of times people reach out to you, and you think, "Well, maybe there's not sufficient covering." I truly believe that in this case, that is not the situation. Yet there is something that God has placed in me that this young man senses I must deposit into his spirit.

I thought about him, and it led me to think about Pastor Ken Taylor. For years, his connection to me was an occasional e-mail here or there, a phone call sporadically, staying connected all because of a word that was dropped in his spirit years prior. And I thought about the vastness of the connections that we have with people, and how sometimes we minimize who we are because we don't understand that our connections go further than the people who are geographically around us.

Especially for a pastor—and I say this as I pray it will bless the lives of leaders and pastors who will read this for years to come—I believe that when God gives you a voice, you cannot categorize the voice you have or the effect you have on others' lives based upon the number of people you may be preaching and talking to on a week-to-week basis. Technology and the ability it gives us to view other people's ministries is powerful. But I think that if it is not kept in its appropriate context, it also lends itself to distortion. It may lead those who are truly effective to fall victim to the feeling that they are not as effective as someone else, because their platform is not as large or as exalted or as magnified. And we who are in the Kingdom of God have got to pull ourselves away from these measures of success and effectiveness.

I was reading on Twitter today as one of my colleagues was tweeting to young preachers, young pastors. He was tweeting very profoundly, and then he said, "Find someone who has been successful."

And I wondered in my spirit how that would be received by the average person reading it. What man calls "success" is not always success in the eyes of God. "Success" has to be put into some context so that we don't ruin people and force people into thinking that they must compete with everybody else in order to get out of them what God has placed in them.

You are only called to do what you are called to do, and you have got to move yourself to the place where you really understand that your effectiveness can't be measured from someone else's platform or someone else's spot of prominence. If you don't have that, it doesn't mean that you are less; it doesn't mean that you don't have. There are people admiring you who may not ever come in contact with you again. They admire your light.

The Scripture says to let your light so shine before men that they may see your good works and then glorify the Father who is in heaven. You have got to move to the place where you embrace the brightness of your own light. The brightness of your own light, you don't hide it under a bushel. You don't hide it under a tree. You allow your light to shine. You believe that to whomever God allows your light to shine, it becomes an edification to them and a glorification of God.

It came into my spirit as this young man was writing to me and texting me, it became real to me that I am not his pastor. He's not asking me to pastor him. He's saying to me, "I need you to consider *mentoring* me," which means there is something this young man sees that has caused him to be drawn to His anointing upon my life; *His* anointing upon my life.

It's not our anointing. It is His anointing, and we must keep that in perspective. It's not our ministry. It's not our church. It's His church. It's His call upon our lives. It's His hand that leads and guides us. It's truly His voice that is amplified even when we speak. What we've got to do is become confident in the fact that God chooses whom He will.

I wish that we could take a spiritual view, that we could look in the spirit and see how interconnected the Kingdom of God really is. It is not denominationalized. It is not fragmented. It is not covered up and segmented and segregated, as we have made the church. There is an interconnectivity in the Body of Christ, within the Kingdom, that causes us to not be able to look at each other with disdain. We all need each other; we all need each other. We must be confident and comfortable enough to yield ourselves to those who need us.

I'm not this young man's pastor, but there's something in me he needs. You and I may not be first, but we must be able to embrace the fact that we're next. When we embrace the fact that we're next, we don't really need first-place status. See, when you grab hold of the fact that what's coming for you is better than what's been, you don't become anxious. You look down the line to realize that there are many, many others in front of you. Hundreds of people are standing in line, hundreds of people standing in line in front of you, before you. When you recognize you're next, you don't become overly anxious or even so zealous that you cannot stay focused on what you are assigned to do in the Kingdom of God or called to do in the Body of Christ. You focus on what God is saying, and you lift your hands, and you don't doubt, because you understand that God says you are next.

There is a difference between "first" and "next." Even within the confines of organizational structures, many people are trying to jockey, push their way up to first assistant, first administrator, first vice bishop. We could just run the gamut of all of the titles. None of that really means you're next, because you can be vested with the second man's anointing and never be qualified for first. Sometimes some of the greatest men are the men who assist the one who's in the top position. But their ability to assist is not an automatic invitation that they should one day lead. I can be great at carrying out someone else's directives but lousy at hearing from God myself.

I love the spirit of Jonathan. The spirit of Jonathan is the spirit that I believe is equally as important as the spirits of Samuel and Saul. Samuel was the one who stirs up and appoints, speaking prophetically. Saul was the one who was supposed to mentor but then becomes an enemy to God. Thus he is an enemy to the plan of God and an enemy to God's choice, David.

I am appreciative of the spirit of Jonathan because Jonathan knows that his right is to be the next king of Israel. He is heir apparent. As heir apparent, Jonathan is getting ready to take over at any moment in the absence of his father, Saul.

Somewhere along the way, Jonathan comes into a sense of reckoning. Jonathan says, "I'm never gonna be king over this nation." So then he transitions from heir apparent to protector of who's next. The church would be better off if some folk who are trying to be next would discern, "Okay, I'm not next, so let me become protector of who's next." When Jonathan makes up his mind to protect David, David's ministry goes to another dimension. David can focus on what he is assigned to do and not be so worried about his number one nemesis.

Any man of God in leadership, any woman of God in leadership, whether in ministry or secularly in the corporate arena, has got to have a Jonathan. Somebody who is clear, "I will never be who I'm protecting, and my goal is not to be them. My goal is to make sure that they can ascend to their rightful place." Which means the spirit of Jonathan can't be a spirit that is birthed from some sense of jealousy. Jonathan can't be jealous. Jonathan can't spend his time jousting. Jonathan can't be no jive talker. Jonathan must focus in on the fact that jealousy, jousting, and jive will cause him to mishandle his assignment.

You've got to find somebody who is assigned to you and who is comfortable with his assignment to you. Not looking for another assignment, not trying to do something else, not swayed by the opinions of everybody else. He just recognizes that, for this season of his life, he is assigned to you. When you find that person with the spirit of Jonathan who is assigned to you, he will help you.

On the way to worship one night, I received another text message from a pastor who would not have any clue, any idea about certain situations that are going on in my life. He said, "Bishop, I'm concerned about you and I'm praying for you."

Now when people say that to you, you can take it, or you can ask, "What's going on?" I wasn't just going to take it and say, "Praise the Lord, thank you," because I wanted to know. I said to him, "Okay, are you sensing something?"

And he said, "Yeah, we're connected and I'm really carrying this."

I thought to myself, "Okay ..." Then I told him—I'm very transparent—"All right, I just wanted to know, because I thought maybe you had heard something that I ain't heard or something going on that I don't know anything about."

And he said to me, "Bishop, no, but I need for you to know that there is an uproar behind the efforts that have gone forth to purposely keep you down. There is an uproar in this city, because folk who are now seeing that certain people have purposely tried to keep you down are no longer silent."

Now I had never had a conversation with this brother about nothing. For one, I had just met him, and I'm not like some people. I don't spill all of my life in my first encounter with people. So I'm just being the bishop and he's being the pastor. And he says, "I'm praying because this thing, I'm seeing it."

I read the text to Lady Marshall and said, "How would he even know anything about this?"

And the spirit of Lord spoke to me and said, "If you be quiet, I will fight your battles. God will fight your battles. You don't have to go out saying, 'This one did that and such and such said this; they trying to do this to me.' If you hold your peace and let the Lord fight your battle, victory shall be. It belongs to the saints."

I texted back to the man of God, "Thank you, continue to pray for me."

Which made me acutely aware of something: there's somebody praying for me and I don't even know their praying, because I don't know what they know to pray about.

The more I look at the life of David, the more I look at the ministry of Samuel to David, the more I look at the relationship between David and Saul, then the more I see that I must bring into some sense of perspective the dysfunction in our beloved king, David.

It starts in his house, the house he grew up in. Let me say it again. A lot of his dysfunction started at home. A lot of the stuff you're trying to get over now so you can do ministry, you can trace back to home. It don't mean you weren't raised in a good home. It don't mean you did not have a good environment. Every family has some dysfunction. Sometimes the dysfunction is that you were given everything. You didn't really have to work for nothing, and now when it's time to work for something, you don't know how to work. That too is a level of dysfunction.

So what we have to do is bring ourselves into some sense of understanding that David is like he is because Jesse was the kind of father he was.

This has been an awesome day for me. I've been challenged with a couple of things, but I've been blessed. Today I was leaving the barbershop with two of my sons, and Dr. Churn stopped us. He was talking to us and marveling at my sons, just marveling at how they've grown.

I introduced Third to Dr. Churn, and Dr. Churn said, "Okay, come here, let me talk to you. Now are you going to preach?" So of course Third gave his response. Dr. Churn said, "I'm just asking. We don't call preachers. I'm just asking. Because what I don't want you to do is wait until you get old and you don't have the benefit of your father. Your father can help you like no one else can."

He said, "Nobody's gon' protect you like your father. Nobody's gon' give you the ins and outs like your father. He's gon' tell you the details. You don't want to wait 'til he's gone or he's so old he can't impart and pour into you. You want to be able to get that. So I don't want you to wait until you just passed age and he told him he said cause don't nobody want to hear you when you get but so old noway so you gotta go ahead and get it and hit it when you're real hot."

And so then my other son, the younger one, the baby, he comes out of the barbershop perky. He just got a haircut, feeling real good, smiling. He walks into it and I said, "Dr. Churn wants to ask you a question." Dr. Churn asked him and my son gave his answer.

Dr. Churn said the same thing to Carlton. "There are things you won't be able to get from nobody like you can get from your father. So you need to be able to glean from your father. Just make sure, whatever you do, that you're honorable in it and that you do it with some passion. You don't have to preach, but your daddy's an awesome preacher, your daddy's an awesome teacher, so there's something in him you gotta glean to become what you're going to become."

Something's going on in Jesse's house. The more I look at 1 Samuel 16:11–12, the more I'm convinced greatness cannot start just when you encounter someone haphazardly. The road to greatness starts in your mama and daddy's house.

Let me tell you what the beauty was in that encounter with Dr. Churn, because this is what was so interesting. My daughter Taylor was standing behind the boys, waving and saying, "I'm gon' preach! I'm gon' preach!" At ten years old, she's saying, "I'm gon' preach!" He wasn't asking her, but there's something that you get based upon where you live. You better watch where you lay your head. I'm serious. You better watch where you lay your head, because where you lay your head has a whole lot to do with what comes out of you.

Let's look at the text. The Bible declares, "And Samuel said unto Jesse, Are here all thy children?" (1 Samuel

16:11). Are here all thy children? What makes Samuel ask this question? He is clear on his assignment. God spoke to him and said to him, "How long are you going to mourn Saul, whom I have rejected? Go down to Jesse's house and anoint the next king." So Samuel is clear that God sent him to Jesse's house for one specific reason, and that's to pour oil on the next king.

I take it seriously every time I get a microphone in my hand, every time I'm sitting with somebody in a one-on-one encounter or on the telephone. When you give me opportunity to pour into your spirit, I do take it seriously, because my job is to find who the oil is for. The church has got to mature. What we've done is poured too much oil on people who look the part but were not assigned. We've got to bring ourselves to a place where we stop looking upon the outward countenance of people and using that to judge what we think they ought to be. You are more than what you look like right now. I may not look like it, but I'm next in line.

Samuel asks Jesse, "Are these all your children?" Because, you know, he almost pours the oil prematurely. When Samuel saw Jesse's son Eliab, he thought, "Surely the Lord's anointed one is before him. But the Lord said unto Samuel, Look not on his countenance, or on the height of his stature; because I have refused him" (1 Samuel 16:6–7).

Part of the problem with what goes on or went on in the house where you lived is that whenever you're chosen, you have to learn how to exist around people who have been refused. Let me tell you something. God has dealt with me so powerfully on this. A large part of what we are dealing with are sibling rivalries with unholy parentage. An unholy father will pit his sons against each other and sit back and call it sport. But a holy father will teach his sons not just how to coexist, not just how to cohabitate, but how to respect who's next. A holy father has sense enough to know he ain't gon' always be around. And if I'm not here, y'all listen to who's in charge.

For my sons, Third, Justin, and Carlton, when they're at that house, ain't gon' be no confusion about who's in charge. Who's in charge is the one I say is in charge when I exit the door. Sibling rivalries exist in ministry. We got unholy fathers, and we got holy fathers who don't like to watch sons fight and call it sport. My daddy ain't never talked about my brother Alvin to me. He ain't never come to me and said, "You know, there's something wrong with Alvin. Alvin is this and Alvin is that." You want to know why? Because parents who are holy recognize that if they don't teach siblings how to love each other, then when the parents are gone, the family is divided.

Look at your neighbor and tell your neighbor, "We cannot fight one another." No, we cannot be trying to jockey for a position. Trying to flex muscle. Trying to see who's the greatest.

The truth of the matter is, when Samuel goes to Jesse's house, Jesse brings everybody before Samuel but David. It's a clear indication of how the father sees his son. You better ask your daddy how he sees you. Ain't nobody gon' tell you the truth like your daddy. This is not to negate mothering, but this is not about the mothering spirit. You better ask your daddy what he thinks about you, how he sees you.

I got sons and daughters in this ministry who will periodically stop by and ask me, "We okay?" I'm not an immature father. I understand what they're asking me.

What they're saying is, "How do you see me?" Because daddies give identity.

Let's look at this. And Samuel said unto Jesse, Are here all thy children? And he said, There remaineth yet the youngest, and, behold he keepeth the sheep" (1 Samuel 16:11). Period. Which means that's all Jesse said. "I got one more, but I don't let him do nothing but watch the sheep, and they tell me he don't do too much of that. His brothers have reported to me that every time they go out there, he's got his harp, singing a song."

David was a psalmist. He didn't wait to become king to start writing. He started writing when he was watching the sheep. Which means the greatest part of David is not the warrior. The greatest part of David is the worshipper. If you let worship be first, whatever comes next will be successful because worship is first. Gotta be a worshipper first.

David worships first. Every time his brothers see David, he's looking at the sheep and talking about "The Lord is my shepherd, I shall not want." Can you imagine what the mindset must've been of somebody who would say, "The Lord is my shepherd, I shall not want"? Maybe he was hungry. Maybe he had been promised some food, but because his brothers were jousting, jiving, and jealous, they didn't bring it to him.

I can prove in the Scripture that they were at least jealous, because in 1 Samuel 17, when Jesse sends David down to the battle with food for his brothers, David is hesitant to leave the battleground. Eliab, his oldest brother, tells him to get back on his beast and go. David says, "What's the problem?"

And Eliab says, "You got that look in your eye like you're about to get into something. Get away from here."

Whenever somebody watches you become what he didn't have power to become, that's automatic grounds for jealousy. David was not a warrior yet. He was not old enough. He was stuck at home. Part of Jesse's having to answer to God is what he didn't see in David.

Kind of reminds me of Joseph. The bible says that Joseph shared his dream with his brothers, and they hated him yet the more. He shared his dream with his father, who should've been able to cover him. But his father, even though he knew that what Joseph was dreaming was real, rebuked Joseph for his dream. If you can't share your dream with your daddy, who can you talk to? And you can't share your dream with your daddy if all your daddy is saying is what he's doing to compete with your dream.

Let me say it again.

"Daddy, Daddy, I hit a home run!"

An absent father says, "Oh, boy, that ain't nothing. I hit about twenty-five home runs when I was your age."

A good father says, "I saw it. When you lifted the bat, I knew a home run was coming."

"And Samuel said unto Jesse, Send and fetch him: for we will not sit down till he come hither" (1 Samuel 16:11). We will not sit down until greatness gets here. What you just paraded in front of me can't be what God sent me here for, because this looks like what He rejected.

That's the problem with trying to be somebody's imitation. If God had wanted somebody else, he would have kept that somebody. A dude said to me—and he was real— he said, "We coming; we just want to make sure when we get there, it ain't gon' be a repeat of what we left." The world says that imitation is the greatest form of flattery. Don't imitate to the extent that people can't distinguish you from what you're imitating. If you are just a carbon copy of something rejected, you can't be next.

I'm pouring into you. I'm giving you all I am. But don't be a carbon copy of me, because me doing me only works for me. You gon' have to find what works for you. And a lot of what's gon' work for you is not what I did. Especially the stuff that equals my mistakes. If you're making my mistakes, you haven't done nothing. The truth of the matter is you learn just as much from my mistakes as you do my successes, and I'm gon' make sure you learn, because I'm gon' keep telling you. *I make mistakes.* I'm not perfect. I mess up. I slip up, and if I don't stay prayed up, I operate in flesh.

I was trying to add up some of the stuff I used to say, and the Lord said to me, "You gotta answer for some of that foolishness." That stuff wasn't right. I know it wasn't right. When it was coming out, I knew it wasn't right.

I'm not teaching you not to be respectful. I'm not teaching you not to honor. I'm teaching you to be spiritual enough that you discern where God is. People are sitting in bound situations because somebody won't give them a position. You ain't got to worry about a position given or a position taken. All you got to do is know when you're next. Know when you're next.

I believe that God keeps it so that we have to stay close to Him. This is our great aggregation, this is our great organization, and to some of us, He says, "You are My assistant. You are closest to Me. You have been proven to be a faithful and supportive person. So when I'm absent, I can give you a directive and you get it done. You stand in My stead, you give My directives, you are in line—but you are not next."

The Dichotomy Between Samuel & Saul

Now what has to happen is everybody in this line gotta be sensitive. I believe God puts "next" sometimes in an unambiguous place, and other times in an inconspicuous place so that "next" won't try to kill the assistant. I'm gon' go off the scene one day, and God gon' call who next. That person gon' be the leader. As for my Jonathan, my assistant, you were good for me, but you may not be good for who's next. He gotta be able to find someone good for him, because the loyalty you have may not be for him.

See, that's why the church is messed up. We think "assistant pastor" means "next pastor." In the sixties and the seventies, maybe that stuff made sense, but this is the twenty-first century. God's pulling, handpicking, finding, and what you've got to do is be so connected to the voice that no matter where you are in the line, if God says now, you're next.

I may not be first, but I'm next. I'm not first, but I'm next. Where is that boy that keeps the sheep? Because we ain't sitting down 'til he gets here. Look at what the Scripture says. "Now he was ruddy, and withal of a beautiful countenance, and goodly to look to" (1 Samuel 16:12). You've got to know how to discern all of that. There was something about David that wasn't quite king material, but he was kind of cute. He wasn't no ugly boy, he just wasn't polished. You know how some of us used to look. You know you pull out your old pictures and put them up against how you look now. The Bible says that the Lord told Samuel, "Arise, anoint him." When next gets there, the oil flows.

Some people are struggling now, trying to do something with what was, because what was won't appoint what's next. I was talking to Bishop Henry Hearns out of Los Angeles, and he was talking to me, and we were just sharing, and he said, "Bishop, have you met Dr. Jack Hapherd?"

And I said, "I was introduced to him at your consecration."

He said, "That's right. You were coordinating my consecration. But have you met with him?"

I said, "No, sir."

He said, "Well, I need to have lunch with you and Jack Hapherd. Jack Hapherd retired, you know, and he looked at me and said to me, 'Henry, I don't want to call you stupid, but you're stupid.'"

Jack Hapherd said that because he's retired and living. Bishop Hearns, on the other hand, is seventy-eight years old and still pastoring.

Y'all, come on. Hear my heart. America, hear my heart. America, listen to me, because I'm serious. It is not just about age. It's not an indictment against age, but it is very much about sensing timing. If your time is up, Suga Ray, sit down. Muhammad Ali, sit down. Bret Favre messed up a stellar career. Want to know why? He didn't know when to sit down.

The day is gon' come when I'm gon' have to sit down. I'd rather sit down than have to lie down. Enjoy some time. Enjoy some of your days. Have some moments where you can sip coffee, go to what's called brunch. We African American Pentecostals, we don't know nothing 'bout no Sunday brunch. Why? Because we been in church all our lives. Sunday school, morning worship, broadcast, evening worship, afternoon choir anniversary, HTU—y'all know what I'm teaching. We don't know nothing 'bout no Sunday brunch.

But there's gon' come a day when I'm gon' want to do brunch. Which means I'm gon' call my kids and say, "What y'all doing?"

"Daddy, we at church."

"Oh, okay, I'm sorry. It is eleven o'clock. Excuse me. I was just thinking about y'all."

"What you doing?"

"Sitting on the veranda, watching the beach, waiting on room service."

We're the only people who think we supposed to wear out. You need to go and relax. Find some comfort. You deserve it. Don't wear yourself out, wear yourself down. I ain't got y'all's energy, and I'm not gon' try to have your energy.

We've got to come to a place where we feel like there's no shame. I read an article that was posted on Facebook, entitled "The Inner Wars of Pastors." I read that article and said, "This thing is so real." I'm ready to hit some pinnacles and some high points and do some stuff that's gon' benefit me in my tomorrow.

I was supposed to be preaching in South Carolina yesterday, 'til they couldn't meet the obligations. I ain't running up and down the road no more, spending out. No. You're not gon' put no value on who I am? *No.* I did that when I was younger. All I ask for is two rooms, you can't do that? You were supposed to pay for my gas, you can't do that? Then what you need to do is invite somebody local. I have made sacrifices to make people comfortable. When I didn't have it, I found a way. So now you want me to drive four hours and preach for you? I may not be first but I'm next. I'm next.

Where is he? Watching sheep. Go get him. We won't sit down 'til he gets here. Oh, this is him. God says anoint him. People can hate on you all day, but when the oil is on you, it's just on you. I don't believe that we should spend time trying to defend ourselves before people who can't recognize the oil. When the oil is on you, it's just on you, and you can't change the fact that the oil is on you. You can't let people minimize that. I love them just the same, but call me when you're ready.

The Lord said, "Arise, anoint him: for this is he." Which means everything that passed Samuel before was not it. *This* is it. May not be first, but I'm next. Man can give you a position and then turn around and take it from you. You'll lose your mind if your only identity is locked in the position. But when you know who you are before the title comes, stripping of the title doesn't minimize who you are.

When you have the spirit to serve, and you serve, and you know that you're doing the best you can, and people sometimes overlook you, you just keep doing the best you can. Don't ever feel like you need to make yourself be seen or make somebody pay attention to you. Whatever is on you, God's gon' make it recognized.

Teenagers go through the phase where it's all about the outward appearance. But God has placed something inside them, and the focus after a while goes to the inward man. And then you will start really experiencing some serious challenges.

I pray for you all. I read your stuff on Twitter. I know how to discern what's real and what's just off the cuff. You think these li'l friends out in the street turning on you is something? Wait 'til God starts using you. Wait until you come into yourself. Wait until that voice that God has given you wakes up and God starts to use you. You ain't seen no haters like the ones that are coming next. So I'm telling you now. Master it with the li'l street friends, because you got a battle coming with the church folk that is unlike anything that you have ever seen in your life.

Man, I didn't know. I'm telling you. I grew up looking up to people, only to realize when I got close to them they weren't as pretty as I thought they were. And I'm trying to keep it real with y'all. I'm trying to keep it real so y'all will stay real. Because I don't ever want you to be disappointed if I do some things or say some things.

I was talking with somebody when the situation with Bishop Eddie Long was in the news, and I said, "Why you got so much to say? That ain't even your pastor." God gave that man a national, even an international platform, but truth of the matter is that it's in that local congregation if they choose to stay with him. You can just turn your TV off. When he comes on, if you don't want to hear him, just turn off your TV. You ain't no member there.

You ain't called to the whole world. That's gon' be a rude awakening for some of these people who think they are wonderful when they wake up. Just because God gave you a mega-ministry don't mean you are called to the world. You are not called to the world. You are called to who you are assigned to.

A whole lot of things give you major platforms. Sometimes it's just charisma. Sometimes it's who you know. But a calling doesn't always come with a major platform. There's singing going on in here on Sundays that will put to shame some of the stuff famous folk are doing. It don't mean we're less effective or less called.

When God raises you up, I want you to be confident and comfortable in who you are. Please get comfortable in your own skin. It's the only skin you got. You can dress it up. You can fix it up. But at the end of the day, you ain't no more than who you are.

You may not ever have a title. You may not ever have a position. But that's not what this lesson is about. This is about "I'm next." *Me*, I'm next. Strip me if you want to. Take my title, but I'm next. You can't stop what I'm about to become—next. You can't prevent me from being what I'm about to be—next. Welcome to next!

Chapter 3
God Said You Can Do Better Than This

I don't want you to be a people who play with God. We are high worshippers, high praisers. We got to find a way to get our lifestyles to match all the excitement we put forth in our worship services. We got to find a way to be just as hype about holiness as we are about praise. Because praise don't mean I'm okay with God. It means I recognize him, it means I know him, it means I acknowledge him. It could very simply mean that I feel him for that moment. We must get serious about God. You've got to get serious about God. No time to play.

The dichotomy between Samuel and Saul is where we are going back to. The dichotomy between Samuel and Saul. For the last several pages, I have been teaching about the need for the church to embrace the spirit of and the need for the Samuels in our lives, and even to understand the assignment and the responsibilities of the Sauls in our lives. We have talked about how important it is for us to draw a distinction between the two spirits and also to understand them. When I say understand, I mean embracing in its totality how important this distinction is for the church. I want you to gravitate to this and grab it. The church must become really serious about what God has assigned for us to do.

Now please hear me, and I want you to lock into this. We must know God to the extent that we know our assignment. It's not enough to spend time in the house of God without discovering your specific assignment. Why are you here? What has God called you to do? You have been placed on the earth for what purpose? What is it that has been assigned to your hand?

As soon as we come to understand our assignment and know what it is, we will also come to embrace that our calling and election must now be made sure. The spirits of Samuel and Saul are both necessary for the fulfillment of purpose. You need Samuel to give identity, to give instruction, to give some sense of direction, prophetically speaking into your life from the place you are now. And as much as Saul fails in his relationship with David, Saul is still a necessary component. Sometimes it is out of pain that we are introduced to the positivity of our real passion.

Let me say it again. It's sometimes out of pain that we are introduced to the positivity of our own real passion. Sometimes it's crying that awakens in us an understanding. If this thing can touch me here, then maybe this is what I've been assigned to do. If this has caused me a burden, maybe this is where I should look to operate. It is out of our own pain that we come to identify what it is God wants us to do.

This is why we must learn to embrace the pain of the moment and not look disdainfully at what we are experiencing. Every moment has built into it a purpose. Every moment of our lives has built into it a purpose. For the believer, there are no mistaken moments. There are no chance or happenstance moments.

The steps of a good man are ordered by the Lord. Which means very clearly that a good man who has been assigned by God to do something on the earth understands that every encounter has locked inside it a purpose. We are admonished by the Word of God to be careful how we entertain strangers, for some have entertained angels unaware. A lot of times we don't recognize that a stranger is an angel sent to give further clarity or instruction in our lives and even in our assignments.

"And Samuel said unto him the Lord hath rent the kingdom of Israel from thee this day and hath given it to a neighbor of thine that is better than thou" (1 Samuel 15:28). God said to Saul, "You can do better than this." I don't ever want to get to the place in my life where God looks at what he has given me and decides I am no longer worthy to possess it.

When we talk like this, the first thought that people generally have is a thought of materialism. But I want your mindset to go further than that and to places more important than that, because the truth of the matter is, things come and things go. You can recover things. Prosperity gospel, as it has been referred to, has become so focused on things that people who are believers are literally measuring the love God shows them by the possessions they have materially.

God's love goes further than what home we live in, what car we drive, what name brands we have, what kind of TV we watch. None of that sums up God's love. None of that defines the relationship the believer has with God. But people have minimized the importance of knowing God in His realness to the extent that we spend our time trying to compare what someone else has with what we have determine how blessed we are.

"The blessing of the Lord, it maketh rich, and he addeth no sorrow with it" (Proverbs 10:22). Sometimes you can be excited about a thing, and then when it's time to make a payment, you lose all that excitement. Sorrow has come.

The one thing that I can never become sorrowful about is the fact that He has redeemed me, saved me, and brought me out of darkness into the marvelous light. The more I think about that, the sweeter that becomes. Believers have to come to a place where we don't judge God's goodness or even His blessings in our lives by material factors.

When God speaks to Samuel, Samuel prophesies to Saul that God is stripping him. God rents the kingdom from Saul; He tears it from him.

What God is saying is not that he is stripping Saul's kingship, because Saul reigns for several more years after this moment. What God means is not that Saul will no longer be called king. A lot of folk still carry titles but don't have the grace or the anointing for the title. A lot of people still sit in seats of authority who shouldn't be sitting in those seats. Having a position does not indicate that God has assigned you.

What God means when he speaks directly to Saul in this moment is that "I am removing my hand of favor, and you will now have to operate under your own power." That's a frightening thought. Think about how difficult it is to do what you do with God's hand on you, and then think about trying to do it with His favor removed. That is, to me, more serious than death.

When God says to Saul, "I am giving the kingdom to somebody better than you," God is also saying, "I am no longer going to allow you to abuse the gift I've given you." A lot of abuse is going on in the church. Pastors are abusing people. People are abusing pastors. Gifts are being utilized as bargaining tools, trying to push the church into something because someone with a particular gift wants to do it, whether or not it's particularly the will of God.

There's a lot going on in the kingdom of God. God is saying to us in this hour, "Are you ready? I will find somebody else." We must awaken to this truth. Don't ever get to the place where you believe that God's gotta use you. That's why we gotta stay humble at His feet. God, anything that I do, I want to stay humble enough for You to use me, not to look at me and say, "You have been exchanged."

You ever purchased something that, while you were in the store, you just had to have? Then you get it home, and it if it's a piece of clothing, you look at it and say, "Lord, no." Or it's a piece of furniture you think it's gonna fit in a particular place, and you realize it doesn't, and then you have to go back and exchange it.

I remember in the 1980s, I worked for a company called Sears. I was in college, and I worked in the automotive center. I worked in Sears for a couple of years. Sears had a policy that they would exchange anything, even without a receipt. All you had to do was bring that product to Sears and they would take it back, no questions asked. We were taught a certain code to put into the registers that would print out a paper that the person would fill out. And we would be obligated to give them their money.

I remember when summer hit, people would come in and buy the hard-shell, car-top luggage carriers. I knew those folks used those things. But when they dropped it back in that box, put that flap over, and said, "We want to exchange this," my obligation was to give them their money back.

You don't ever want to get to the place where God takes you to the return counter and exchanges you for somebody better. The one thing I want everybody to understand is there's always somebody better. Don't ever get so caught up in what you do and how well you do it that you think you got a monopoly on doing it. There is always somebody better. There is a better orator than you. There is a better administrator than you. There is a better musician or singer than you. There is a better church worker than you. There is a better Christian than you. So we should never get to the place where we think God's stuck with us. He sent me to tell you, you don't ever want to become so puffed up that He takes you to the exchange counter and trades you in for somebody better than you.

I would go kicking and screaming. I would. I would say, "Lord, please don't turn me in." You remember *I Dream of Jeannie*? Jeannie use to say, "Master, Master, I won't do it again. Please, Master, please, Master." Jeannie understood that though she had the powers, she needed Anthony Nelson to fulfill her purpose. She could blink herself anywhere, but she was bound to her master. You've got to come to the place where you become bound to the Lord. Where quitting on God is not an option. Where walking away from God is not something that you think about or even discuss. Where you become committed to what He's called you to do.

Blessed is the man that walketh not in the counsel of the ungodly, nor standeth in the way of sinners, nor sitteth in the seat of the scornful. But his delight is in the law of the Lord; and in his law doth he meditate day and night. And he shall be like a tree that is planted by the rivers of waters that bringeth forth his fruit in his season ... (Psalm 1:1–3)

You have got to become so committed that you become like a tree. A tree represents being planted right. As

The Dichotomy Between Samuel & Saul

soon as I discover where I'm supposed to be, the next thing that's going to happen is found in that verse: "He shall be like a tree that is planted by the rivers of waters that bringeth forth his fruit in his season." The next thing you're gonna do is prosper. When you're planted correctly, when you are where God wants you to be, the next thing you do is you prosper. You bring forth fruit. You produce.

I was listening to someone recently, maybe it was on the radio or maybe even on television. And this person said, "You don't ever walk by an apple tree and hear it straining to bring forth apples. It's planted and through the process of time, unless it's dead, it will produce."

We're each straining to do some things, and the strain is probably a clear indication that the thing I'm trying to do is not my assignment. No, because when I'm assigned, then under pressure I know how to get it done. Under the worst of circumstances, I know how to get it done. Discouraged, I still end up doing it. Disgruntled, mad, angry saying I'm not gon' do it, yet I find myself getting dressed and doing it again because it's the thing I'm assigned to do.

God speaks to Saul through Samuel and says, "You need to go and destroy the Amalekites. And you need to destroy them because they're trying to stand in the way of my people." The miracle is in the instructions. The one thing we're struggling with more than ever before in the Body of Christ is human ability to follow instructions. God tells Saul through Samuel to destroy them, and His specific instructions are to kill all of them and their cattle. Saul is not to leave anything breathing in that nation.

Saul calls his army together, but as they go, Saul decides he does not want to kill everything. So he allows his soldiers to keep the best calves so that they might offer them as a sacrifice or an oblation for God. When Saul gets himself caught up in trying to run God's business, Samuel shows up again and says, "Saul, have you done what God said?"

Saul says, "I've done what God said, the Lord be praised."

Samuel says, "Then why do I hear cows?"

God has sent me to ask, if you've killed it, why is it still making noise? If you've really put it under your feet, why is it still jumping up at the worst possible moment and interfering with your assignment? If you've truly put down jealousy, why are you still looking side-eyed when people are blessed? If you've really put down envy and even insecurity, why is it so difficult for you to work with everybody? If you've really put down lust, why are you still in a lascivious relationship? If we have truly done what God has said, why is there stuff popping up and waving at us that we were supposed to have killed?

Saul claimed he was doing something really spiritual. Saul said, "We'll save these cows to offer them." I think that Saul was lying, but he told Samuel that the animals would be offered. What is it about us that when God gives us specific instructions, we allow our own minds to interfere with the mind of God? It's a sad moment when we can preach obedience but live rebellion. We can tell everybody else what to do, but we ourselves don't want to become subject to what God has called. The church is filled with people who have this self-righteous attitude wrapped up in an unrighteous body.

God speaks through Samuel and says to Saul, "Your rebellion is a problem." Verse 23 – "For rebellion is as the sin of witchcraft and stubbornness is as iniquity and idolatry because thou hast rejected the word of the Lord he has also rejected thee from being king." When God gives a directive, who are we to change his directive?

Elijah go down to the brook of Cherith, and God tells him, "Stay there; I'll command the ravens to feed thee." But then the day comes when God says to that same prophet, "Elijah, get up and go into the city. I've commanded a widow woman to sustain thee." There's a difference between being fed and being sustained. Feed thee, I'll do that temporarily. But if you obey me temporarily, then I'll put you in a place of permanency. Because the word "sustain" in the Hebrew means that if she never wants, you won't either. The Bible says that every time that widow woman went back to the barrel, there was meal enough for her and her son. Because of the obedience of Elijah and the obedience of the woman to the voice of the man of God both of them lived through the famine, never wanting food again.

And the famine doesn't end. I'm gon' obey so I'll have steak in the midst of the famine. Lobster in the midst of the famine. In the midst of the famine. When you walk, live and operate in obedience, so you are sure to be taken care of in the midst of the famine.

But you got to walk in obedience. There are too many of us not walking in obedience. The opposite of obedience is rebellion. There is no gray area. There's no middle ground. The opposite of obedience is rebellion.

I'll take it a step further. Delayed obedience is rebellion. I've been teaching that the Kingdom is about moments. If the Kingdom is truly about moments, then we can't be delayed in our obedience. The Bible says that when Elijah gets to the city, he finds that widow woman collecting sticks for a fire to prepare her last meal. Had he delayed the moment, had he waited a day, then when he got there, what would have been her offering would have already been consumed. You don't have time to be delayed.

If God tells you to go and pray for somebody, you don't sit home for twenty-nine days trying to figure out whether or not they're going to receive your prayer. God said go pray for them. He didn't tell you to worry about them receiving it. He said go pray. If you delay, in the process of time things happen to them that could have been avoided had you obeyed Him and prayed.

We sit in church, and sometimes the Lord says to us the simplest of things. Maybe God says, "Embrace them." And we'll sit up as if to say, "Not me! No, they're never gon' look at me crazy." If God said, "Embrace them," then your focus ought to be on walking in obedience.

Saul gets in trouble with God because he's a disobedient leader. Disobedient leaders cause nations to suffer. Disobedient pastors cause churches to suffer. Disobedient singers will mess up a choir. How do I figure that? Come to rehearsal. If you don't come to rehearsal, then when it's time for the choir to sing, we end up singing like a quartet instead of a choir. Your disobedience is what's messing us up.

God speaks through Samuel to Saul and says, "Rebellion is as the sin of witchcraft." Saul says to Samuel in verse 24, "I have sinned. For I have transgressed the commandment of the Lord and thy words because I feared the people and obeyed their voice. Now I therefore pray thee pardon my sin and turn again with me that I may worship the Lord."

Verse 26 gets very interesting. And Samuel said to Saul, "I can't church with you no more." You cannot walk in blatant disobedience forever, then decide to turn and think there not gon' be consequences.

See, we got this generation of people who think all they have to do is say, "I'll ask the Lord to forgive me." No. When you really repent, the word "repentance" means to turn away from. Which means repentance is not saying, "I'm sorry." Repentance is *turning away from*.

We were on our way home one night and Taylor said to me, "Dad, I really want to make sure I go to heaven."

I said, "You will."

She said, "But how do I know I'm gonna go to heaven? Because I'm scared to die."

I said, "Taylor, when you give your life to the Lord, you are certain to go to heaven." Then I asked, "Are you saved?"

She said, "I don't know. I don't think so, because I don't know what I did when I was a little girl."

I said, "Well, if you don't know, then you need to be saved. Next time I give an altar call, you need to come to the altar."

She said, "Dad, I don't need to do that, because then people gon' think y'all not teaching me right."

Then she said—and these were her words—she said, "Save me right now."

Now, I know *I* can't save her, but her words were, "Save me right now."

I said, "Well let me lead you to the Lord."

She was sitting in the backseat I was driving in the front seat. I said, "Repeat after me. I am a sinner."

From the backseat: "I am a sinner."

"Lord, forgive me."

"Lord, forgive me."

And we went through the entire thing that I would normally go through with somebody. Then I said, "Now you are saved. What is the first thing I tell people to do when they get saved?"

First she said something about jumping up and down, but when I asked again, she said, "Oh! Tell somebody they're saved."

What blessed me was that I happened to look on Facebook, and Taylor had changed her status. She wrote, "I just got saved. If you believe me, say amen."

You can't keep living wrong. When you really get saved, you turn. You are not saved and you keep doing the same thing. No, when you repent, something's gotta change. Something different has to begin to happen in our lives when we really get saved. You don't automatically stop everything, but you turn in another direction. And when you turn in another direction that means you are now turned toward Him.

Saul played with God, played with Him so long that finally when Saul said, "Come on, Samuel, pray with me," Samuel said, "I can't church with you no more." We have got to get serious enough about God that we say to people, "I'm not gon' keep pulling you out of what you keep running back into."

No, when you repent, something changes. You can't say "I'm sorry" and then pull Scripture: "When I would do good, evil is always present." That's because you ain't turned. Come on, Paul. Wake up, turn. If you turn, then evil will have to find another direction from which to come. Satan trips us up a lot of times because we are so predictable. He knows that all he's got to do is disappoint you and you gon' run back to it. To what? What's familiar. What's available.

Samuel says, "I will not return with thee For thou has rejected the word of the Lord." Can I tell you how detrimental it is for you to constantly hear God speaking and constantly reject what He's saying? It's dangerous. It's dangerous to hear God and constantly reject what God is saying. God speaks; we do what we want. God speaks again; we do what we want. He speaks yet again; we do what we want. When do we become people who do what he said?

I'm not doing what I want. I'm doing what He said. The difference between my life and the life of those who walk in disobedience is that I do what God said. I obey God. By doing what? Obeying His Word.

The bible declares that Saul has rejected the word of the Lord, and so the Lord rejected Saul from being king over Israel. Saul doesn't lose the actual throne. He loses the approval of the One who gives the throne. Nothing is worse than sitting in the seat that you've lost grace for. Nothing is worse than trying to flow in something that you're no longer anointed for. Nothing is worse. To God, Saul is a walking dead man.

Have you ever gotten frustrated because you've heard so many prophecies, and it seems like ain't nothing coming to pass? Then you say, "I don't need nobody else prophesying to me about what's gone happen. I just need it to happen." I know I've said it. Let me tell you what's dangerous about that statement. What happens if God stops talking and you have nothing pointing you to hope?

Prophecy not only reveals God's intentions, but it gives hope to the faith of the believer. It doesn't have to happen today, but if God tells me it's gon' happen, I've got something to hope for. For four hundred years, God gave no open revelation. Can you imagine how dismal that time must've been? Living a life where you can't get to a Word.

Where you can't be told something that will build you up. If God gets silent, what are we gonna do?

I need Him to speak. Lord, if ain't nothing coming to pass in this season, just keep talking to me. Just keep speaking to me. Just keep telling me what's gon' happen. I'll gain strength from Your Word of what You tell me is going to come to pass.

"Samuel turned about to go away, he laid hold upon the skirt of his mantle, and it rent." Saul literally grabs hold of Samuel and tears his mantle. When I read that, something went off in my spirit. After God has rejected them, people will become desperate. They'll start trying to keep the anointed around them whom God is still with, even though they know God has rejected them. It's a dangerous thing to be kept in that place where somebody's trying to hold on to you. You can't be the sustenance for somebody God has already rejected.

Some people are trying to hang around you because His glory is still on you and it's lifted off of them. Y'all better check some of these Lodebar connections you've got—these people you're with whom the glory hath departed from, yet you're trying to maintain friendship with them. If the glory has departed, you might want to depart.

Samuel turned about to go away, and Saul laid hold upon the skirt of his mantle, and rent it. And Samuel said to him, "The Lord hath rent the kingdom just like you tore my skirt. God just tore you away from what it is that He gave to you freely. And not only did He take it from you, but He found somebody better."

God has no respect of person; that's what His word says. But God does have favorites. I know you don't like that. Well, you say you got the favor of God upon you. So God's got favorites. Who are God's favorites? Those who do His will. What makes you favored of God? When you walk in obedience.

"God, whatever You do, don't strip away from me the one thing that differentiates me from everybody else."

"Son, walk in obedience. If you obey I'll stay with you. But if you disobey me, I'll strip you of the Kingdom."

Don't take Your Spirit away. I need Your glory. I want Your glory. Less of me and more of You. That's what I need. Can you say that? Begin to say, "God, I'm sorry for any disobedience that I've operated in. Blatant, clandestine, known, unknown, forgive me, Lord. I need in this moment less of me and more of You. Allow me to walk, Lord, as Your obedient and humble child. For Your Word declares, 'Humble yourself therefore under the mighty hand of God, that he may exalt you in due season.'"

God, I don't want you to find somebody better than me. The only way I'll become disqualified from what You called me to do is if I start walking and operating in myself. God, I yield myself. To whom you yield, that's whom you'll serve. God, I don't want to serve my flesh. I don't want to serve what my flesh is calling for. My flesh calls for a lot of things that I know are not in Your will. So I'm asking now, Lord. Less of me and more of You. That's what I'm asking for. Put my flesh under subjection that I can move, God, according to Your will. Move, God, according to Your plan. I don't want to be in the way. I don't want to be in the way of what You want to do through me.

God wants you to walk in obedience so He can use you. You're God's choice. You're His choice.

Chapter 4
You're about to be Promoted by Jealousy

"And Saul was very wroth, and the saying displeased him; and he said, They have ascribed unto David ten thousands, and to me they have ascribed but thousands; and what can he have more but the kingdom?" I Samuel 18:8).

I want to deal with the subject "Promoted By Jealousy." On August 24, 2011, Steven Jobs, who was the cofounder of Apple, resigned as the CEO of this great American corporation. Everybody loves iPads, iPods, iPhones, all the way across the board. But there is a very interesting history behind Apple.

Steve Jobs had two friends whose names are not as familiar as his; one is Steve Wozniak and the other is Mike Markkula. Steve Jobs and Steve Wozniak were employed by a growing computer company, Hewlett-Packard. As they are working there, Steve Jobs says to Steve Wozniak, "I've got this wonderful idea. I don't know how it can work, but I've got a wonderful idea of how we can possibly put a computer in every home in America."

Wozniak laughs because he is the computer interfacing genius. And he tells Jobs the components, all of the technology that is needed, will not fit into something that can be placed into a home. But Jobs stays on him. Every time Job encounters Wozniak, he says, "Man, listen, I think if we really put our heads together, we can come up with a way to put a computer in every home."

They finally get together and find a way to build what was known then as the Macintosh. They bring in their third friend, Markkula, to help finance and run their new company. They find a market for their product, and the company becomes what is now known as Apple.

This company does extremely well, but in 1985 there is this fierce battle between Steve Jobs, the other cofounders, and the board of directors of Apple. Steve Jobs is ousted from Apple. He loses this fierce fight with the Apple board of directors, and he founds another computer company. He calls it NeXT.

Jobs founds this company in 1985, and when he gets this wonderful company up and going, it becomes such a threat that the board of directors of Apple decides that if they don't become a part of this, NeXT is going to overtake them.

Remember a couple chapters ago, I dealt with the subject "I May Not Be First But I'm Next"?

So Apple goes in, and they offer to buy NeXT. Steve Jobs goes back to Apple and becomes the CEO of the company that put him out. So now he's got the leadership and the NeXT money. It kinda reminds me of former and latter rain coming at the same time.

This is a kind of exegetical teaching without the Scripture. An exegesis of Steve Jobs's life demonstrated experiences that gave a revelation. That's all exegetical preaching is. Take the text, awaken the text, and make the text relevant to the people you're talking to: that's a great exegetical preacher. There are some good topical preachers who can take a topic and work a topic, but if I'm gon' live,

The Dichotomy Between Samuel & Saul 69

I'd rather live out of the Word and not out of somebody's idea.

So Steve Jobs resigned. He's been extremely ill. He has a disease. His resignation, I'm almost certain, is connected to the fact that he needs to put attention on himself. It's not the first time he's stepped aside. He stepped aside a few years ago, but whatever that was went away, and he came back. Came back obviously stronger and wiser, because Apple has done some very interesting things over the last few years. But now he's resigned again.

I received the tweets about his resignation from *The Wall Street Journal*, because I don't just follow people on Twitter. I follow where information is. If you just follow people, all you hear is what they're thinking. Follow news outlets, follow major thinkers, follow people who have accomplished some things. I follow Bishop Jakes. I don't expect him to follow me; I follow him. The problem with some people is that everybody you follow, you want them to follow you. If everybody's following, who's teaching? You ought to be following more folk than are following you. The caliber of people you follow is a great indication of how you think.

I follow *The Wall Street Journal*, I follow CNN, I follow Roland Martin, I follow people who are great thinkers, like Bishop T. D. Jakes. I follow people who understand. I follow apostle Richard D. Henton. He's gotta be seventy-something years old, but I follow him because whatever he says, there's glory on it. And I want that glory. I want that glory. If you really want to go somewhere, just check who you're following. It'll determine where you're going.

So Steven Jobs resigns today. He has a quick understanding. He understands that sometimes in leadership, so much can be going on with you that if you don't remove yourself from the equation, what's wrong with you then becomes what's wrong with the whole organization. Sometimes we miss the understanding that we carry into what we into everything we are. So everything that's good about you goes into everything you're a part of, but everything that's bad about you goes into it too. If what's bad about you is outweighing, outshining, or outsizing what's right about you, then you have become a detriment to anything you are a part of.

Most people don't think that way. When something goes wrong, the first thing we want to do is find out whose fault it is. That search should always start with you. It should always begin with you. If you see something wrong in whatever it is you are a part of, check you first. You can do one or two things: discover that you are a part of the problem and remove yourself, or discover that you are a part of the problem and become an active part of the solution.

Steve Jobs is removing himself. This is not trivial. When Steve Jobs went out and started that company NeXT, he also had enough money to buy the computer graphics division from Lucasfilm. He took that to another level as Pixar. Which means that when you watch *Toy Story*, Steve Jobs gets paid. He ain't just an apple; he's a cartoon.

When Walt Disney Company bought Pixar, Jobs became the largest shareholder of Disney stock because he owned 51 percent of Pixar. Hang around some folks who have something so they can tell you how to get something. We may own our clothing, some of you own your homes, some of you own your cars, but the truth of the matter is you'd like to own more than just your ideas. You want your ideas to put you in an ownership position.

So Steve Jobs steps to the side. Now when I'm looking at this and I'm contemplating our lesson, I immediately think about Saul. I immediately begin to reflect on what Saul could have done to make his life better had he been still plugged in to God. There is a way that God can move you out and move somebody else in, yet you will still be respected and revered for what you've done.

Steven Jobs has resigned as the CEO of Apple. He's stepping aside from the day-to-day leadership to become chairman. The chief operating officer (COO), Tim Cook, now becomes the CEO. Jobs says, "I can't do it anymore." He goes Cook and says to him, "I'm gonna promote you to CEO, which means it's time now for you to duplicate yourself in somebody else as I have duplicated myself in you."

What would it have been like for Israel if Saul had sense enough to know the glory wasn't on him anymore?

What I can do is preserve what it is I was initially sent to protect. Every king is sent to protect the kingdom. Every pastor is sent to protect the church. Every shepherd is sent to protect the sheep. When you lose sight of the fact that you are the protector, then you become the molester of what you should be protecting. I can't have no middle ground. I'm either protecting it or molesting it. And if I'm protecting it, I'm protecting it from everything that can hurt it, even myself.

This is where the difference between Samuel and Saul is awake in my spirit. Saul does not understand that if the glory's not on him, there is still a place for him. Doesn't mean God has left him, it just means He's changed His glory. The glory for what I'm doing now will one day lift. So I've got to invest in sons and daughters who can keep going what I have spent my life protecting. I've got to have sense enough and discernment enough to move out of the way so that I don't become a detriment to what I love.

"And it came to pass when he had made an end of speaking unto Saul, that the soul of Jonathan was knit with the soul of David, and Jonathan loved him as his own soul" (1 Samuel 18:1). When the shift comes, you will sense it. You will sense a drawing to someone other than the person who has been the focus.

It's dangerous when Jonathan starts loving David. A lot of times we think all of Saul's problem, everything that's wrong with Saul, is about David reigning or David growing. But the truth of the matter is that Saul also notices when allegiances change.

Everybody wants to talk about allegiance until folk start showing allegiance to somebody other than who's talking. You want me to show allegiance until my allegiance draws me to something you don't want me drawn to. Then you want to call me a traitor. I'm not a traitor; I'm just following where the glory is, because the only person who can lead me into my destiny is the person who has the glory.

Jonathan's heart is knitted to David's, which means Jonathan, the son of Saul, starts to respect David, and his daddy can't stand it. Watch people. Sometimes the folk who have a problem with you are very much the people who love you. They don't realize who loves them. So they become jealous of your ability to draw people.

Some people have the ability to draw. Some men of God are anointed to draw. I look at the life of Bishop Gilbert Patterson, and long before we knew him, Bishop Patterson in the 1970s was drawing four and five thousand people to his meetings. Billy Graham has the ability. You ain't never heard him holler, scream, twist, turn, or prophesy, but he has the ability to draw. Not just the ability, the anointing to draw.

And so you cannot become jealous when there is something on somebody that you don't particularly have on you. What you do is get up under what's on them and push it. Every good preacher is not a pastor. Sometimes great administrators are just that, administrators; they're not pastors. So you have to really become confident in who you are so that you can be what God wants you to be.

Jonathan's heart is knitted, his soul is knitted. Jonathan is loving on David like he loves himself. Now if anybody was gon' be jealous of David, you would think it would be Jonathan, because Jonathan looks like the one next in line. But somewhere along the way, Jonathan saw a glimpse into his own future, and he saw that being king was not in the cards for him. Sometimes knowing who you're not gon' be is better than finding out who you are, because if you can embrace who you're not gon' be, you'll never try to be something that God didn't call you to be.

Everybody's trying to discover what God wanna make them. No, what we may need to discover is what God don't want us to be. I'll become what I need to become by process of elimination. I ain't supposed to be that, I ain't supposed to be that, I'm not supposed to do that. Ain't nothing but for me to do this.

I follow this lady on Twitter. She is a relationship coach, and I follow her for her relationship points. She said, "There are two places to find peace, and one of those places is purpose." You find peace when you find purpose. You find peace in your relationship and interactions with people when you come to the reason you're in their lives. If I know why you're in my life and why I'm in your life, then as long as I keep that in perspective, there's not really much you can do to hurt me. I know what my purpose is.

Let's look at the text.

Jonathan loved David as his own soul. Saul took him that day and would let him go no more home to his father house. Then Jonathan and David made a covenant because he loved him as his own soul. And Jonathan stripped himself of the robe that was upon him and gave it to David and his garments, even to his sword, and to his bow, and to his girdle.

When you discover who the glory's on, you ought to be willing to give him everything you got. When you sense where the glory is, you ought to be willing to turn over everything you have. Jonathan gave David his robe. That's just not somebody giving a coat. Jonathan's robe indicated his role. You get that? His r-o-b-e indicated his r-o-l-e. So when he gave up his r-o-b-e, he said to David in essence, "My role is whatever you tell me I am."

If I trust you to lead me, then what Paul says in Galatians, chapter four, is that I would even pluck out my eyes for you. What Paul is saying is when I was really truly leading you, you had no need for your eyes. My eyes were your eyes. Sheep, sheep, follow shepherds. Sheep without a shepherd are lost sheep.

"And David went out whithersoever Saul sent him and behaved himself wisely." That's a good adjutant Scripture right there. David went out whithersoever Saul sent him and behaved himself. Don't let me send you as an emissary and you act a fool. It reminds me of what I was taught as a child: don't show out nowhere, but especially at somebody else's house. Most believers in the Kingdom would be killed if we were ambassadors to other countries. The other country wouldn't kill us. The country that sent us would kill us.

To be an ambassador means that you have literally given yourself in the service of somebody else. An ambassador doesn't represent him or herself. An ambassador represents the one who sent him. What we've got to discover is how to be real ambassadors for Jesus. Every time you go, you're going by virtue of He who sent you; no more I but Christ who lives in me. I'm an ambassador of Jesus Christ on the earth.

The Bible says of David that "Saul set him over the men of war, and he was accepted in the sight of all the people, and also in the sight of Saul's servants." I think that's really interesting. It is the promotion by Saul that draws people to the anointing of David. That's how David becomes strong. He doesn't become strong because he is trying to outshine the one who sent him. When the anointing is on you, it's just on you.

Several years ago, HBO did a special and it was called "Sisters in the Name of Love." There were three singers: Patti LaBelle, Dionne Warwick, and Gladys Knight. Everybody talked junk about Patti LaBelle because in every song, it looked like Patti was taking over. After watching it about nine hundred times, I came to this conclusion: Patti wasn't taking over. Patti was just being Patti. If I'm out there and everything I do is out there, you can't push me in. Patti's livelihood is Patti LaBelle. She made her money as Patti LaBelle. The money I know of is Patti LaBelle money.

Sometimes you hang around people, and if you talk about how good you feel about yourself, they want to say, "You always full of yourself." No, I just like myself. And I'm not gon' stop liking myself because I picked a few friends who don't like themselves. Stop belittling yourself because you're around people who don't know who they are. You know who you are, then go ahead and know who you are.

The people are drawn to the anointing of David. And the truth of the matter is that David had to deal with this even in his own daddy's house. His brothers had problems with him. When they were at the forefront of the battle and David was about to leave, he looked over and asked, "Why isn't there anybody fighting?"

They said, "David, please go home, because you always start trouble."

David said, "Y'all come to watch it, I come to do it."

There's a difference between the people who are anointed to watch it and the people who are anointed to do it. There are a whole lot of Monday morning quarterbacks who ain't never played a game. "He should've done this, he should've done that." You wasn't even a good Pop Warner quarterback but you know what an NFL quarterback is supposed to do?

I refuse to live my life as a Monday morning quarterback behind somebody else's successes. I'm going out and making some stuff happen myself. Some people, all they can talk about is what somebody else is or is not doing. But put them in a corner and ask, "Now what have you done in the last thirty days? You've accomplished what in the last six months? You've gone where?"

Some people ain't never had as many folk saying happy birthday to them as they've got now with Facebook. Now they got nine hundred birthday wishes. Before Facebook, it was three people—their momma, their daddy, and their sibling.

The Dichotomy Between Samuel & Saul

The Bible says that David went out and he did whatever Saul sent him to do, behaving himself wisely. Saul set him over the people and the people started to gravitate toward David.

It came to pass as they came when David was returned from the slaughter of the Philistines that the women came out of all cities of Israel singing and dancing to meet King Saul with tabrets, with joy and with instruments of music. And the women answered one another as they played and said Saul has slayed his thousands and David his tens of thousands. And Saul was very wroth ...

Every good daddy ought to want his children to do more than he's done. So what's wrong with Saul's spirit that he can't celebrate the people recognizing the success of David?

First, Saul wasn't a good daddy. A good father wants his children to do more. I got my daddy's name. I've done some things to make his name shine. I've done some things to make his name look bad. But in all those things, he's never stopped, as my daddy, telling me what I can become. When I was doing things to make his name shine, he wasn't sitting back with his arms folded, mad. When I did things to make his name look bad, he didn't shy away from me and act like he didn't know me. As my daddy, he stood. "Good, bad, or indifferent, I'm attached to that boy and he got my name." Sometimes he may have gone home and wondered why he didn't name that boy something else. But he never said it to me. He never gave me a look like me having his name was a problem.

Watch daddys who only want you to have their name when you're shining but then want to act like they don't know you when you're struggling. Watch daddys who cannot celebrate the name they gave you, even if that name is getting more recognition than theirs. You got to be careful that you don't hang around folk who can't stand your name. A good daddy celebrates the name of his children. Sonship is what everybody should be after, regardless of gender. Watch a daddy who despises the name.

I can be talking to somebody who'll say, "Yeah, I ran into Carlton," and I'll smile. Hearing that name makes me smile. You've got to get to the place where you love what you gave birth to. Good, bad, or indifferent, ain't nobody gon' make me despise my children.

Second, Saul did not understand the power of succession. Succession is not something a pseudodaddy dangles in front of sons to control them. Succession is not something that a pseudodaddy uses to put one son against another. A real daddy knows that every son gon' get something. So you don't have to play sons against each other. In the whole scheme of fathering, every son is important. All twelve tribes have significance.

Third, David is finding himself through the lostness of his daddy. So even a bad daddy can leave a legacy. Even a bad one. Even a bad father gon' leave something. Every daddy, good or bad, right or wrong, strong or weak, gon' leave something.

Saul can't understand succession, because if he understood succession, he would be celebrating that as long as we keep duplicating what the people need, they gon' serve this kingdom. People keep coming because their needs are being met. Every pastor in the world ought to wake up to that. People don't just keep coming because they like you. They can always find somebody they like. People keep coming to a place where their needs are being met. They're not gon' go too many seasons without their needs being met. Because when their needs are no longer being met, it means something else has taken over the atmosphere.

I can almost guarantee you that Saul was more angry that the women stopped looking at him. Isn't it interesting that the women start heralding David's strength, and women literally become part of David's struggle? Every good preacher has to be spiritual enough to turn back the hearts of certain people, because people can be too drawn to your charisma.

That's why a real, true man of God won't let you put but so much glory on him. The more you celebrate me, the more loaded down I become that I need to give this glory to God. If I don't give it to Him, then I'll start acting like I did something for you, and I ain't did nothing. Everything you got, you got from God. Even the Word I preach that blesses you ain't my word, it's His Word. I'm just somebody He's using. It's robbery for me to take His glory to myself.

A preacher can get a woman if he don't turn that affection back to God. The affection has to be turned back. You give somebody something they've never had, and it affects them in a way they've never been affected, then the first thing they want to do is respond in flesh. A man of God with any spiritual insight says, "Don't let me take advantage of this. Let me turn this heart back to God." The heart needs to be turned to God, not to the preacher.

David didn't hire these women to sing that song. The women just started singing. They made up the song. They wrote the song. They put it in A-flat and they started singing. Saul has slayed his thousands, David his tens of thousands. It probably started out real slow 'til it got to the African American women, and they put a li'l beat to it.

Promoted by jealousy. The whole of the lesson is that Saul never loved David like he could have and should have. Everything that ever happened between Saul and David was Saul using David for his own purpose. Saul used David to kill Goliath. He never asked him, but nowhere in the Scripture do you see Saul saying, "Son, go sit down. You're too young." The first thing Saul said was, "Get my stuff, put it on him, and send him on out there."

When an evil spirit would come upon Saul, the Scripture says that he would send for David, and David would play on his harp until the spirit left Saul. Saul's role in David's life is constantly perverted because Saul only sees David for what David can do for him. He never sees David for what he can give to David.

Saul does introduce David to a lifestyle he's not accustomed to. And you can't give people a certain lifestyle and then take it away from them and expect them not to tell your business. You can't fly people all over the world in private jets and put them up in plush hotels and then cut them off without expecting them to respond. They going to go off. That's why you got to be careful who you give stuff to. They gon' show out. Stuff ain't gon' slip out—they gon' tell it. They'll show out on you in the worst possible place.

You're going to be promoted, even if it's by somebody else's jealousy. Somebody else being jealous of you may be the stepping stone of your promotion. Let them be jealous and you get promoted. You just keep your heart pure. Keep your spirit right. You be found doing what God wants you to do.

Chapter 5
The Difference is in His Anointing

This series of teachings that I have broken down into five distinct chapters are set forth to help the believer come into an acute awareness that when you are God's choice, no weapon formed against you shall prosper. Weapons will form, but weapons cannot prosper.

The more anointed you become, the more you will face the formation of Satan's weaponry designed to keep you from the fulfillment of the assignment upon your life, and thus from your place of destiny. The weapons are formed for the express purpose of putting distractions and deterrents in the way of the believer's destiny. Satan's goal, his ultimate desire, is to distract us, because once we are distracted, we're out of focus on the vision that God has given us by way of assignment.

Distraction is not just about your gift, not just about your ministry, not just about what you are assigned to do by man; distraction is designed and put into play to bring the believer away from the salvific message of Christ. Paul rehearses that message when he says to us, "His grace is sufficient." The sufficiency of God's grace is enough to carry you past any distraction.

So what we have to do is focus on the sufficiency of the grace of God, and not allow even the things that Satan might magnify or amplify to become such a distraction that we go in an opposite direction. Satan wants to get you off the track you're on and put you on a track to nowhere. And if the enemy can get you off of the track God has assigned and put you on a track to nowhere, he'll let you run a long time like that.

There a lot of people with a whole lot of strength, a whole lot of energy, and a whole lot of opportunities, but they're on roads that lead to nowhere. If the enemy can distract us to the extent that we are no longer on the road that God put us on, then it matters not how hard you work, it matters not how much time you put in, it matters not how many people admire you—if you're not on your destiny track, then you will not please God.

Grab this and put it in your spirit: there is no such thing as a permissive will of God. There is no such thing as a permissive will of God. God has one will; it's His perfect will. And if we are not in His perfect will, we are out of His will. People sometimes act like they think, "I'm in the permissive will of God. God's permitting me." No. If God had a permissive will, then that would mean He's giving permission for you not to be on. And God never gives us permission not to be where He told us to be. His grace is sufficient, but He does not give us permission to be off. So if you're not in His perfect will, then you are not in the will of God.

There is no such thing as a permissive will. If there was a permissive will, there would be a permissive Word, because the Word of God is the expression of His will. There is only one Word. If there was a permissive will, then instead of God saying to us, "Come out from among them and be ye separate"—which is His Word, which is His perfect will—he would say, "Well, if you can't come out, just do the best you can." There is no place where God gives us permission not to be where he told us to be.

If there was a permissive will, then when God said to Adam and Eve, "You can eat of every tree in the garden but this tree," what would the consequences have been? When they ate from it, God would have said, "Oh, that's all right. If y'all would've turned the page, you would've found out that when you eat of this tree, it's gon' be okay. I'm gonna really let you eat of it a couple of times until you come to understand it."

If there was a permissive will, then parents would have a permissive attitude. Not a one of us who are real parents have a permissive attitude. "I told you not to do that. Okay, you gon' go ahead and do it anyway? Well, don't worry about it. Just ignore what I said earlier." And we want God to be the God who says to us that's it's okay for us to miss Him?

But when you are fixed and no longer satisfied with being distracted, you begin to say, "God, what are the things I need to do to be in the center of Your will? I want to be where You want me to be, even if Your will for my life in this season is for me to just be quiet. Lord, show me how to be quiet. Let me study to be quiet."

There is no permissive will of God. And if we don't grasp this, we're always going to give excuse for distractions. We've got to get this thing out of our minds that there is a place that we can go in God where everything we say really contradicts Him. There is a permissive doctrine found in Catholicism. It's called purgatory. Purgatory is a place you can go to fix everything you didn't fix here on earth, before it is determined whether you go to heaven or hell. That ain't in the Word. There is no purgatory. You don't have a whole lot of time. It is appointed unto man once to die. The perfect will says it's appointed unto man once to die, and after death judgment.

"There is therefore now no condemnation to them which are in Christ Jesus, who walk not after the flesh, but after the Spirit" (Romans 8:1). Paul does not say, "There is therefore now no condemnation to them which are *almost* in Christ." Permissive will means I ain't really got to be all in, just enough in for Him not to knock me out. His grace is what keeps Him from knocking us out, not His permission for us not to be in. "There is therefore now no condemnation to them which are *in* Christ Jesus." If I'm in the house, I'm in it. If I'm in trouble, I'm in it.

"There is therefore now no condemnation to them which are in Christ Jesus, who walk not after the flesh, but after the Spirit." Flesh is always looking for permission to be fleshy. But when you're in the Spirit, the Spirit compels you to walk in wholeness in Him.

I see now why the doctrine of permissiveness is popular for this generation. We want to be permissive members of churches and we want to be in permissive relationships. I got a friend request on Facebook a few weeks ago, and this person had in her relationship status, "in an affirming relationship." So before I accepted her, I typed a message and I said, "Could you please explain to me what this is?"

She said, "Oh, don't worry about it. It's just to throw off people. Most think when I say that, it means I'm in a gay relationship, but I'm not."

We're in a generation where people are in a whole lot of stuff and want permission to be in it. In sin, but still want to be labeled saints. When you're in Christ, old things are passed away. When is the last time something old passed from you? Because when you're in Christ, old things ought to be passing away daily. Nothing new can come until something old go. We want to be new without getting rid of the old.

The saints and the church of God have to move to a place where we stop acting like it's all right to be permissive. "For the law of the Spirit of life in Christ Jesus hath made me free from the law of sin and death" (Romans 8:2). In my flesh, I'm under the law of sin and death. When I'm in flesh, every law attributed to sin and death is at work in me. When I'm in sin, sickness and disease can grab me, emotional instability can grab me.

But when I'm in the Spirit? This is why the Bible teaches us that when the enemy comes in like a flood, the Spirit of the Lord lifts up a standard. A standard is a banner. When you're in the Spirit, the banner comes up and says to the enemy, "You can't breach this territory." Which means when sickness and disease—high blood pressure, diabetes—are coming in like a flood and you're in the Spirit, the Spirit lifts up a sign that says, "You, sickness, cannot lodge here. You, disease, are not welcomed here."

We talked about the women celebrating David and Saul. The issue was they ascribed to David more victories than they gave to Saul. Saul has slain his thousands; David his tens of thousands. The text then goes on to tell us, "And Saul eyed David from that day and forward."

I need to watch who's watching me and figure out why. "Why you keep looking at me?" If you were from my generation, you would preach from that subject. "What you looking at?" You need to watch who's watching you and then discern why they're watching. The Bible says Saul eyed David. You need to really look at that word "eyed" to get an understanding of what it means. It means Saul was fixed on David, because Saul saw in David what Saul missed.

The root of jealousy is when somebody looks at you, wants to be you, and comes to the conclusion he can't be you. And let me put this in your medulla oblongata, your cerebrum and the cerebellum of your mind, down in the cortex of your brain. Nobody is jealous of you other than the folk who are insecure about themselves. You're never jealous when you're all right with you. When you're all right with you, you can look at somebody with all of it and be all right. "You might be wonderful there, but I'm the only one of this. Nobody else can carry this. Nobody else can be me. You can't beat me being me, so I'm okay."

We've got to move to the place where we learn that jealousy is birthed out of insecurity. Saul eyed David. Saul had his eye fixed on David, which meant from that point Saul stopped living his own life and started living vicariously through David. You'd be surprised at the number of people who are living their lives vicariously through somebody else. Watch a parent who's always in his child's business. I'm not talking about a twelve or thirteen-year-old child, I'm talking about a child of thirty or forty. The parent is all in the child's marriage because he ain't got one. In his child's relationship cause he ain't got one. If your child comes home upset about something on the job and you call the job, there's something wrong with that. You got an adult child and you all in that child's business? If that child is grown enough to get the job, that child ought to be grown enough to handle whatever issues come with the job.

But some parents lose themselves and started living vicariously. Like a mother sees a guy, and then looks at her daughter and says, "Oh, you ought to date him." My parents ain't never run out and said I ought to date somebody. They either gave approval or shook their heads silently at who I brought home. But they didn't go get nothing and bring it.

That's Sampson's problem. Everybody talks about Samson and his first wife and everybody talks about Samson and Delilah, but the truth of the matter is that Samson's insecurities and Samson's issues with women started with his daddy. The Bible says Samson saw this woman down in a place called Timnath, and he saw she was good to look upon. The next thing he did was ask his daddy go get her for him. His daddy ought to have looked back at Samson and said, "You want her, go get her for yourself."

You can't live your life through somebody else. *Get a life*! Everybody ought to get a life. When you get a life, you won't be eyeing somebody else. I would hate to be a new person going into a church. I think this one is pretty okay, but I would hate to be a new person going into some places. People will eye you up and down. Bernie Mac said a li'l boy came downstairs and when Bernies told him he couldn't have no cookies and milk, the li'l one looked at him and looked him up and down. Now children are looking you up and down like they gon' jump on you.

Get a life! Stop eyeing other people. When your eyes are off other people and your eyes are on Him, you know very little about what's wrong with other folk. People will stand up and testify, and you'll think, "I did not know you were going through that. Oh, my Lord, I had no idea." It's not that I'm insensitive to my brothers and sisters, but I'm not all up in your Kool-Aid.

"And it came to pass on the morrow that the evil spirit from God came upon Saul." Because the anointing, the anointing makes the difference. God will allow certain things to take place so he can put you in place. Every hurt isn't Satan. Sometimes God causes the pain to come so you will move. We're giving Satan credit for the hurt when the truth of matter is sometimes the spirit comes from God. Right here in the text, the Bible says the evil spirit came from the Lord. There is another portion of Scripture that tells of a lying spirit that came from God. God sent a lying spirit and put it in the mouths of the prophets.

You've got to watch. Sometimes God will allow there to be dissension so He can get certain folk out of your life. God says, "I'm getting ready to make y'all fall out," so He can get them away from you and you away from them. Sometimes He will allow you to find out that somebody is not your friend. We spend all our time hurting over what God orchestrated.

The Bible says that this evil spirit from God came upon Saul, and he prophesied in the midst of the house. What do we do when the prophet is full of the Devil? That's why you got to know the Word. Know the Word of God. When any prophetic word does not line up with the Word, the Bible tells us to try the spirits to see whether they are of God, because many false prophets have gone out into the world. You've got to watch and make sure that what's being said is in the Word. Does it line up with the Word?

The Bible declares to us that Saul got this evil spirit on him. Prophesying and angry. Prophesying and mad. Prophesying and hurt. Prophesying and confused. Prophesying and jealous. Prophesying and insecure. Prophesying and sick. You want what comes to you to flow from a place of purity.

That's why any good preacher, even when we're going through something, we've got to put aside what we're dealing with and let what flows through us flow through purely. I think every preacher is accused of using the pulpit to throw off on people. Some preachers really do that. But

I tell people all the time, "You can't accuse me of throwing off on you if I've already confronted you about what I'm saying. I'm not throwing off on you, I'm just preaching about something you did."

Throwing off is if I don't ever talk to you about the issue. If I'm trying to resolve the matter from the pulpit instead of between us, that's throwing off. If I said, "Hey, come in my office. I need to talk to you. Such and such was not what you should've done. That was in error," and then I got up and preached about it, that ain't throwing off. That's me warning the whole house not to be like you. And if you don't talk so much, the whole church won't know I'm talking about you. If you put on Facebook, "I see I was preached on today," then everybody who was at church gon' remember what was said and say, "Oh, that was you."

Church 101: the Word hits all of us. How we handle just depends on whether or not we are mature. Don't fall out with the vessel; I'm just carrying the mail. Your check supposed to come on the first and the mailman don't deliver it, don't jump on him. Go call the people who were supposed to ensure the delivery of the check.

Saul prophesies, and while he's angry and prophesying, the Bible says, "David played with his hand as at other times and there was a javelin in Saul's hand." I want to talk about the subject "What's In Your Hand Determines Who You Are," because you can't fight and build at the same time. You're either gon' carry a javelin or you're going to carry the instrument through which your anointing works.

David's instrument of anointing at this particular moment is what he plays with. "David played with his hand as at other times." He's anointed to soothe the evil spirit on Saul. What do you do when what's in your hand doesn't match what's in your enemy's hand? If what's in your hand doesn't match what's in your enemy's hand, then the last thing you need to do is fight. You gotta take what's in your hand, work it, and let the anointing make the difference.

I want to suggest to you that the harp in David's hand is more lethal than the javelin in Saul's hand. Why? Because when you've got the instrument through which your anointing works, you can send the enemy back to the dry places of the earth. Goliath had a sword; David had a sling and five smooth stones. What David had in his hand, he was anointed to use. If you can find what you're anointed to use, you can defeat an enemy with weapons of mass destruction.

I know everyone wants to make themselves big and bad. Even I will try to fight my way out of a situation. If somebody try to back me in a corner, I'm sure I'll swing. When they find me, something's gon' be in my hand. If somebody take me down, then somebody gon' take me down, but under my fingernails or something there's gon' be some DNA. You ain't just gon' beat me and I don't do something. I'm gon' swing back. I'm gon' pick up something. I'm gon' try to find something to pick up and get me out of this situation. But if I'm up against somebody who is a fighter, chances are I'm going down.

I'm not really a fighter. But put me in a room with somebody across the table and let us debate. Very few people can outtalk me. Very few people have the gift of gab that I have. I can be wrong and almost make you think I'm right. You can have facts, and I can look at you and say, "But you need to look at this." And I'll do it calmly. Let you get all your frustrations out, all your emotion, and I'll say, "Hey, but I want you to look at this."

Why? Beause talking is where my anointing is. I'm crazy to go out swinging. If I'm gon' beat a man, I need to beat him in a room on opposite sides of the table where we can discuss it. "Come now, let us reason together" is my Scripture. You better know where your anointing is.

My anointing ain't singing. Every now and again the spirit to sing may come over me and get me through a song. When that song is over and the anointing lifts, I wonder, "Who was that?" But singing is not where my anointing is.

Some of y'all are trying to operate where you're not anointed. An anointing can come on you to get something done, but being anointed to do it is a different thing. The anointing can come on you to bake strawberry cakes even when you ain't really no baker. But the anointing will come on you to bake them only until God sends an anointed baker. When He sends a baker, what you will discover is baking a strawberry cake is not as easy for you anymore. You ought to be spiritually sensitive enough to recognize, "Wait a minute, why am I trying to do that? Sister Marilyn is here, and she bakes the best strawberry cakes that anybody has ever tasted."

A lot of people want to be licensed and credentialed as prophets. Just because the Lord used you to give a word don't make you a prophet. The Spirit can come on you to give a word, but that does not qualify you to be a prophet. There's differences between the spirit of prophecy, the gift of prophecy, and sitting in the seat of a prophet. Three different dimensions of prophetic order. The Bible says that after Saul had got caught up with the witches of Endor, he went and got caught up with a company of prophets. He started prophesying just like them, but he was not a prophet. The prophet was Samuel. Samuel sat in the seat of a prophet. The spirit to prophesy simply came upon Saul at times. But Samuel sat in the seat of a prophet.

Samuel is the prophet. Nathan is the prophet. David is king. David is worship leader. But David is not prophet. When God needs to send a word, He sends the prophet.

I was picking my son Carlton up from an event one evening and it dawned on me that last time I was in my office, my phone light had been blinking and I had not checked my messages. So I called in remotely from my cell phone and checked my messages. A gentleman had left me this message, saying, "Bishop Marshall, great man of God, my name is Prophet Castle. The Lord has given me a word for you." Prophet Castle is a Caucasian brother. He left his number and asked very kindly if I would call him.

So as I'm waiting on Carlton, I call this prophet. When he answers the phone, I say, "This is Bishop Freddie Marshall from Winston-Salem, North Carolina, and I'm trying to reach to reach Prophet Castle."

He says to me, "Praise God, Bishop Marshall!" And he begins to prophesy to me.

He told me the Lord woke him up and said to find Bishop Freddie Marshall. He said, "I did not know you, don't know anything about you, never seen you." Now, you all have seen me operate in the prophetic, but it was a different anointing. Somebody being in your presence and prophesying is one thing, but God dropping your name and somebody calling you all of the way from Florida? God will send a word, and He'll send a word that's specific to you.

First thing out of Prophet Castle's mouth was, "Because you are a bishop in the Lord's church, may I prophesy to you?"

I said, "You sure can prophesy to me, certainly."

He said, "The enemy has come for your ring." When he said that, he had my attention. He said, "God said your

The Dichotomy Between Samuel & Saul 93

ring is the sign of your authority. So Satan has come to try to strip you of your authority." He began to prophesy. The man prophesied all up and down my life. He prophesied until literally I was in tears, because everything he was saying was of God. Everything he said was of God.

God wasn't through. Prophet Castle sent me a text message. He prophesied on Monday everything I experienced in California on Thursday, Friday, and Saturday. He said to me, "Every move of God has come out of you, the planting of ministries has come out of you, the establishment of your apostolic order has come out of you. For the next season of your life, God says He is getting ready to send a wind that will start from the west and travel to the east. This time, God wants to blanket the whole nation."

Part of the prophecy he gave was, "God says it is time for you to seek rest. Everybody around you needs to be sensitive to the need for rest." I wish I could share some more; I can't remember all he said. But he texted, "Good afternoon. We pray that you are rested and refreshed today and that God is moving in a mighty way in your life as well. Was just sitting at my desk praying and God spoke to me and told me to text you this. Conquering regions in apostolic territories is a part of your apostolic mantle and the spirit of the Lord said that he is now opening the Orient and the far eastern countries of the world to that mantle you wear. We love you, Bishop Marshall."

This is how amazing God is: I had just gotten off the telephone from a long conversation with Bishop Summerville in Africa. He said to me, "Bishop, if you can't come, can you send somebody? We just need somebody with your mantle in our nation."

This is not about fluffing up Bishop Marshall; this is about the prophetic order. This is about what God is saying. If the aura of that anointing is on me, everybody under my mantle ought to carry it. The folk in Africa are saying, "If you can't come, can you just send somebody who has your mantle?"

Real sons and daughters can't be ashamed to grab the mantle of the fathers they're under. Because when you go, folk ain't looking for you. They're looking for what you're attached to. You ought to be grabbing mantles. You ought to be saying, "I'm going where he was. I'm taking the dimension he just left." Folk ain't got to die for mantles to be transferred; somebody just got to be promoted. Elijah was taken up, and what he said to Elisha was, "If you see me when I'm taken up, you can have my mantle."

When you carry the mantle of a father, you wear it. And what you've got to learn to do is how to put it on you so it'll fit you right. You got to carry it. A mantle is not a piece of hardware. A mantle is a coat. When you put the coat on, you walk in the authority of the one whose mantle you have. You've got to get to the place where you understand how significant it is to be up under a mantle that you are not ashamed of.

What's in David's hand works for him because the anointing is on it. What is the anointing on in your life? You can use it anywhere. If the anointing is on your voice, just start singing and watch demons back up in the atmosphere. They try to tell you you can't get no help, you can't get financial aid, then just start singing in the financial aid line. Because everything standing in your way is a distraction and deterrent from Satan.

Sometimes I can be sitting waiting on somebody to make a decision on something that I really need done, and he'll look like he's not doing it. All it got to do is quicken. When I quicken and shake my head, it's coming in my

The Dichotomy Between Samuel & Saul

favor. It's gon' turn in my favor. He'll say, "You know what, I don't know why we gon' do this, but we gon' go ahead and do it." And I'll be looking at them thinking, "I know why—because I shook in the atmosphere, and the anointing that's upon my life made Satan get up off of you."

The Bible declares that Saul has a javelin. Saul has what worked for him, but David has what he's anointed to do. So he plays, as other times before he has done, and the Bible says that as he played, Saul cast the javelin.

When you're effective in what you're anointed to do, expect the attack. Anything you're called to do ain't gon' just happen. From the time of John the Baptist until now, the Kingdom of God has been under attack, but those who know their place in the Kingdom keep pushing to take it by force. One of the things that I hear the Lord saying even now is that we've got to come from this defensive mode to the offensive mode, because the assignment on our lives is to take territory. Part of the problem is you're trying to defend the li'l island you've got, and God wants to give you a nation. Stop sitting on the island trying to protect it—build you up an army and go and conquer other lands. Be like Alexander the Great in his great conquering.

Historically, we are told that Alexander the Great spent the last twelve years of his life in pursuit of other lands. He was thirty-something years old when he died, and he was so focused in pursuit of other lands that when he died, he died in Alexandria—but not the first one. He kept going, and every place he went, he named Alexandria.

Deliver me from these cautious saints. That's why we have territorial wars in ministry: because people don't know how to move to their next assignment. You still guarding the broom committee. You started sweeping before we had anybody else. Brooms are kept in the closet, and you standing at the broom closet like a sentry at Buckingham Palace. You know what's so sad about that? We done graduated to a vacuum cleaner, it's all the way on the other side of the building, and ain't nobody even trying to get in that closet. It's a shame for the shift to come and you don't know it's shifted, because you guarding what we don't even use no more.

Saul throws his javelin at David because when you are effective, Satan is coming. The Bible says, "And Saul cast the javelin; for he said, I will smite David even to the wall with it. And David avoided out of his presence twice." The Scripture tells us to resist the Devil and he'll flee. Part of our issue is we're trying to cohabitate with the Devil. You are trying to live with the Devil, you are talking about the Devil getting on your nerves, but you keep feeding him. You keep giving him permission to do what he does, to be who he is. David avoided him.

You can't just be anointed to function; you have to be anointed to exist even around dysfunction. An anointing to function is one thing. An anointing to avoid dysfunction is something totally different. Wherever there is function, there is also dysfunction trying to take out function. So you got to be anointed not only to sing in the choir, but you got to be anointed for the non-serious choir members who come late, who come chewing gum, who come and play. Nothing worse than when somebody playing in what you're passionate about. So you can't just be anointed to do it. You also got to be anointed to put up with people who act like they want to do it, but you know they're not passionate. And when you're anointed to do it, you don't quit because your committee is sometimes stacked with non-passionate people; you get anointed enough to infect them with your passion. Because when you're truly anointed, you're gonna either run people off or draw people in to that anointing. They become those who want to be up under the mantle.

The bible says "And Saul was afraid of David." Why does Saul fear David? The difference is the anointing. Saul, every time he looks at David, is reminded of his own missed opportunities. That's really what's wrong when people we have been in connection with seem to be doing better with somebody else. You have to have respect for the anointing that is on someone to be able to draw out of people.

I remember when Bishop Pressley came and preached here six or seven years ago, because it was such a blessing to me for him to speak these words. What he said came as he looked at Michelle, who had just moved here. Now, Michelle is his niece, his sister's daughter, so he's known her all of her life. He looked at her and realized that coming here was what she needed to come into herself. Helping her come into herself wasn't his assignment; it was the assignment for here.

You can't get mad if God is using you to plant and somebody else to water. I helped her; I'm the one taught her how to pray. Okay, but now she knows how to pray. Am I gon' hold that over her the rest of her life? People say, "You know you wouldn't know how to pray if it wasn't for me." Truth of the matter is, you may have taught me what to say, but trouble taught me how to pray. I'm teaching you the Word, but trouble will teach you how to find it. I'm giving you Scriptures, but trouble in your life will teach you how to apply them. All I'm doing is planting; trouble will water it. But in all of it, God is the One who gives the increase. You can't be jealous when God uses somebody else to do what you couldn't do in a person's life.

Pastors, hear this: you don't own members. Members are not slaves bought on an auction block down in South Carolina. Members are sheep who belong to the pasture of God, who are supposed to be the ones who help bring forth the great harvest. I've had to see a lot of good folk walk away, but nothing blesses me more than when they look back and say, "Bishop, look at where I am." You are where you are because something I said help propel you, but I can't negate what the man you're under now is doing to help develop you.

Kingdom leaders don't get jealous. Only church people get jealous. Kingdom people don't get jealous. Kingdom people say, "Doing what? Praise the Lord!" I don't have a son or daughter I don't celebrate. I can tell them about themselves and still celebrate their successes. I don't get jealous over their successes. I'm not jealous over your success. I want you to become.

Saul is jealous of David because of closed doors. After every missed opportunity is a closed door. Better watch how you treat people. If that door closes, you don't know what you gon' be able to do. What if your help is the last person you hurt, and you can't say "I'm sorry"? What if your hope is the last person you wounded or offended? Receive people back with open arms, because that could be the answer. This is how the world says it: be careful how you burn bridges, because you don't know what bridges you gon' have to cross over.

Every time Saul looked at David, he also looked at closed doors. Every time David walked in the room, Saul heard doors slamming in his life. Ain't nothing worse than having to watch your replacement replace you. Nothing worse than watching your replacement when the glory used to be on you. Now when you say move, don't nobody move. When your replacement says move, everybody move. If you're not careful you'll be trying to do what it's time for your replacement to do, and you can't fake the anointing.

A good replacement is up on you. Not to irritate you, but because a good replacement recognizes when it's time for you to move on, he's got to be in place. So every time you turn around, there's your replacement. Every time you look around, there's your replacement. You talk junk and they smile at you. You done turned other folk against him, but he keeps loving you. Because a replacement ain't threatened by your insecurity. Anointing makes the difference.

Every now and again you ought to go home and check yourself and say, "Lord, is it still with me? Because if I'm trying to do it and your glory ain't with me, then ain't no need in me trying to do it."

Every time Saul sees David, Saul recognizes a need to repent, but he doesn't any longer have the capacity to repent. Pride goeth before destruction, a haughty spirit before a fall. When Saul gets lifted up in his own pride, he no longer can hear when God tells him to repent. He can no longer identify the fact that he has become reprobate. When you become reprobate you're still flowing like God is with you, but He is not.

David, when he gets into his tenure, has this great fall with a woman by the name of Bathsheba, who later becomes his wife. After that fall, David writes in Psalm 51, "Create in me a clean heart, O God; and renew a right spirit within me" (10). Purge me. If you keep on reading, he writes stuff like "Lord, take not thy spirit away from me." Because David recognizes that sitting on the throne with a crown and a robe is not what really secures his kingdom. What secures his kingdom is the glory of his anointing. When the anointing is on you, the anointing makes the difference.

The Bible declares that Saul was afraid of David because the Lord was with David. The Lord who was with David is the same Lord who had departed from Saul. If you're next, if you're the one that the glory is on, the last thing I want to do is make you my enemy. Saul should've recognized that the glory had departed from him, that God had moved on, and that David was now His choice. Saul should've been wise enough to sing "Remember Me." Or he should've started singing a hymn that I think has been misinterpreted:

Pass me not, O gentle Savior,
Hear my humble cry;
While on others Thou art calling,
Do not pass me by.

That ain't talking about blessings, y'all, that's talking about service. When Fanny Jane Crosby wrote that song, this is what she was saying, in the vernacular of this generation: "Whatever You do, Lord, in this season, please, Lord, don't do it without me."

I find myself praying that prayer more and more. Whatever You're doing in this season, please don't do it without me. There is nothing worse than having been in the middle of where God is, only to walk in one day and find you're on the outside, on the periphery of where God is with no access to get in. It's almost like being high in the Spirit, feeling the presence of God, and all of a sudden you come in church and you can't feel nothing. Everybody around you is feeling the essence and the presence of God, yet you can't feel anything. You feel no glory.

I've been there. I don't know if anybody else can admit it, but I've been there. Where folk were praising God all around me, not just jumping and shouting and dancing but worship was in the atmosphere, and I was standing around almost as if I couldn't even identify with the moment. There is nothing worse than when His spirit departs.

Saul lost what David gained. The dichotomy of Saul and Samuel is very much this: Samuel grew with the move of God; Saul blocked it. Samuel remained relevant; Saul lost his relevance. Samuel kept his ear to the mouth of God; Saul used the last conversation he had and tried to live for years on that word.

When the Scripture declares, "Man shall not live by bread alone but by every word that proceedeth out of the mouth of God," there is a progressive word of God. Which means God himself is not finish talking about His creation. Therefore, we have to remain on the cusp of what God is doing and not get so arrogant in our last point of reference that we think we know where God wants us to go. I'm seeking you, Lord, for direction for my next move, for my next decision, for my next step, because if You don't tell me what it is I'm supposed to do, God, I'm not gonna know what to do.

Begin to say, "God, give me direction. Show me where you want me to go. Show me what it is I should be doing in this season of my life." Whether your relationship with God has had no interruptions, no distractions, and no deterrents, or you're just getting back into the flow of your relationship with Him, it doesn't matter. We all need to begin to say,

> Lead me, guide me along the way,
> For if You lead me, I cannot stray.
> Lord, let me walk each day with Thee.
> Lead me, oh Lord, lead me.

That was the first hymn I learned to play when I used to take piano lessons and I had to play a recital piece: "Lead Me, Guide Me."

We've got to be sensitive. I've been around the Lord a long time, and what's so wonderful about the relationship is that I still don't know everything there is to know about Him. So I got to handle my relationship with care and concern. Show me, Lord; I want You to lead me and guide me along the way.

> Savior, Savior,
> Hear my humble cry;
> While on others Thou art calling,
> Do not pass me by.
>
> Let me at Thy throne of mercy
> Find a sweet relief;
> Kneeling there in deep contrition,
> Help my unbelief.

One hymn can carry me a week. The anointing, His anointing, makes the difference.

About the Author

Bishop Freddie B. Marshall, Ph.D. preaches a strong and declarative message of Grace and repentance, admonishing all to embrace their individual process of growth, maturity and awareness in Christ. As a man of faith, Bishop is an example that if you believe God, you are assured to receive whatever you expect.

His time as a student in the local school systems of Winston-Salem Forsyth County School System, his alma mater North Carolina Central University in Durham, NC and the recipient of several earned and honorary degrees, certifications and recognitions has prepared him to remain a relevant voice to the Kingdom across several decades of church leadership and transition. As a trained and educated episcopate he is an apostolic voice of preparation, a proficient Catechist who is sought after nationwide as an instructor, trainer and mentor.

As an author he has penned several works that are currently used to assist ministry leaders in their continued service to the modern church. Bishop Marshall has received his M.Div with an emphasis on Organizational Management and Church Leadership from Southwest Baptist University. He has also earned a Ph.D. in Cognitive Studies from The New Charter University.

He enjoys life with his wife Mrs. Azaviea Brown Marshall, who has brought healing and wholeness into his life. He is the loving grandfather of one granddaughter, with another grandchild soon to arrive. He is proud of his sons who are all ministry servant leaders and his god-daughters, who have all developed their own relationships and identities with The Lord Jesus Christ.

www.ingramcontent.com/pod-product-compliance
Lightning Source LLC
Chambersburg PA
CBHW020234170426
43201CB00007B/424